MW01453976

Flak Bait

EIGHT DECADES DODGING FLAK AS A BOMBARDIER,
FBI AGENT, TRIAL LAWYER, AND TEXAS MAVERICK

by
James P. Simpson

and
Geoffrey Leavenworth

EAKIN PRESS Waco, Texas

*This book is dedicated to Connie
and to our children, Simone, Scott, Jamie, and Greg.*

FIRST EDITION
Copyright © 2007
By James P. Simpson and Geoffrey Leavenworth
Published in the United States of America
By Eakin Press
A Division of Sunbelt Media, Inc.
P.O. Box 21235 🖰 Waco, Texas 76702
email: sales@eakinpress.com
🖳 website: www.eakinpress.com 🖳
ALL RIGHTS RESERVED.
1 2 3 4 5 6 7 8 9
ISBN 978-1-934645-21-5
ISBN 1-934645-21-4
Library of Congress Control Number 2007937483

Contents

Foreword by Michelle Sierpina vii
Introduction by Liz Carpenter ix
Author's Note and Acknowledgments xi

The Early Years
What's in a Name? 3
Too Poor to Paint 6
Cheaper by the Half Dozen 9
Momma Knows 12
The Copperas Cove Crony. 14
The Saga of the Relief Shirts. 15
The Texas Centennial. 16
County Meet. 19
Entrepreneurship 21

The War
An Encounter in Los Angeles. 25
Lana Turner and Me in Palm Springs. 29
One a Day in Tampa Bay 31
Aboard the *Ile de France* 35
The Irony of War 43
The Battle of the Bulge 50
Homecoming. 54

    From the German Front to the French Riviera 56
    France Revisited 63
    My Friend Manuel 65

College Years
    Entering UT 73
    The Water Was Cold But the Rock Was Hot 75

The FBI Years
    Telegram from J. Edgar Hoover 81
    The Ten Most Wanted 86
    The Deserter 88
    On the Trail of Communists in Minnesota 91

Galveston and the Rackets
    A New Life and Bride in Texas 99
    Why I Opposed Organized Crime 104
    The Campaign 106
    A Bribe Offered 111
    The Runoff 113
    After Defeat—the Beginning of the End 116
    The Isle of Vice 124
    The Balinese Room and the Texas Rangers 126

Fifty Years of Law Practice
    Defending Motherhood and the
       Right to a Public Education 145
    A Decade of Free Dry Cleaning 148
    High School and the First Amendment 150
    Banking at the Sailor's Retreat 152
    Starting College of the Mainland 154
    Death on the Highway 158
    Madalyn Murray O'Hair 161
    A Tranquil and Steady Dedication 163

Appendix
"Three Men Who Cracked an Empire,"
 The Texas Observer, June 14, 1957 173
Campaign Speech, James P. Simpson, Candidate
 for County Attorney, Galveston County
 Democratic Primary, July 25, 1954.................. 177
"Padlock on the Balinese," *The Houston Press*,
 June 10 and 11, 1957............................. 182

Foreword

Find a comfortable spot, turn off the phone, sit back, and prepare to become intimately acquainted with a fascinating array of characters and their stories. You will chuckle, you may cry, and you will certainly laugh out loud as Jim Simpson, storyteller extraordinaire, recounts his lifestories with riveting realism. Jim displays the wit of Will Rogers and Mark Twain, the sensitivity of Viktor Frankl or Martin Buber, and the unassuming, *aw shucks* charm of the Texas country raconteur.

Jim introduces his life through the eyes and ears and eccentricities of the famous, the infamous, and everyone in between. His reflections as a young man flying bombing missions in World War II must be read by everyone who has a vote in every nation in the world. His look at the activities of the criminal element in the 1950s reminds that courage, persistence, and integrity can triumph over evil. His love of family, from his devotion to his mother in Copperas Cove to his adoration of Connie and their family serves as the finest role model of family values and personal principle.

Several years ago, Connie Simpson persuaded her husband to join a life story writing group because his life comprised so many amazing stories. Lovingly, he accompanied her, although he was reluctant. Despite himself, he wrote and shared his stories, surprised at the awestruck reaction as the other group members soaked up his every word. With time his writing evolved and became even more authentic and compelling.

We owe collective thanks to Jim Simpson for generously offering readers his head full of memories, his heart full of compassion, and his soul's window on four score and more of life on this planet.

—Michelle Sierpina, Ph.D.
Director, Osher Lifelong Learning Institute
University of Texas Medical Branch
Galveston, Texas
June 2007

Introduction

From the skies over France and Germany to Chicago's gritty south side, Jim Simpson has defended our nation against the tyranny of foreign dictators and organized crime. But the most remarkable aspect of his life story may be his quiet defense of our Constitution right here at home. Against school boards and civic leaders who thought that pregnancy undermined a girl's right to a public education, that the right to publish a newspaper does not extend to high school students, or that an atheist can be deprived of her Constitutional right to free speech because of her unpopular beliefs.

These are among the toughest battles because they must be fought against fellow citizens, neighbor against neighbor. Of course, these threats are posed by people who stridently believe in America, but who think that the views of the majority take precedence over the rights of the minority, if not the rule of law altogether. Protecting our Constitution requires daily vigilance, as today's headlines make only too clear.

In his corner of the world, Jim Simpson has provided that constant vigilance. I wonder if he and his brand of citizenship can be cloned?

These pages are part of a rich literary tradition—the memoir. How do you write a memoir? Find your scrapbooks, your snapshots, and a typewriter, computer, or even an old quill will do. If you are in your eighties, find a young kinsman like Geoff Leavenworth, with a fresh memory and nimble fingers and get going!

Don't edit as you go. Chronological order helps. Birth through education, jobs, marriage, children—work time and play time—until you are done. Now all you need is a publisher like Eakin Press, with an experienced editor like Virginia Messer, and there it is—your life and times. Now all you need is a snappy title like *Flak Bait*, and you have a book. Your eight decades of dodging flak as bombardier, FBI agent, trial lawyer, and Texas maverick are open to the world.

You'll be proud and glad. I was.

>	—LIZ CARPENTER
>	Author and former press
>	secretary to the late
>	Lady Bird Johnson

Author's Note and Acknowledgments

Two events helped shape this memoir. First, I was influenced by the story of John Bradley, who never spoke of his war experience and whose son discovered his role at Iwo Jima only from the contents of boxes of old photos and letters. The son, James Bradley, recounted his father's experience in the bestseller, *Flags of Our Fathers*. While I was never as reticent as Bradley, I also found myself reluctant to talk much about my war experiences in the years immediately followed the Second World War. I realized that I didn't want one of my grandchildren to discover some of my old photos or letters someday and have to try to piece together what I did in England, France, and Germany.

Second, my wife Connie and I had the good fortune to begin taking classes at the Osher Lifelong Learning Institute at The University of Texas Medical Branch in Galveston. I had done a fair amount of writing in the practice of law, but our work at the Institute was different. We were writing our stories—for ourselves and for our classmates. With encouragement of my family, I began to collect this writing, and eventually, we considered the possibility that the stories might amount to a book. From the outset, Connie, a former FBI stenographer, helped me get the stories on paper. And my daughter Simone and her husband Geoff, a writer and ultimately my co-author, pitched in with editorial and production assistance. My son Jamie helped collect the archival photos, so it really was a family affair.

I will always be grateful for the inspiration and instruction offered by Michelle Sierpina, the founding director of the Osher Lifelong Learning Institute. Without her guidance, this memoir would remain merely a collection of memories. Connie and I were also privileged to study under John Gorman, professor of literature at the University of Houston-Clear Lake and also an instructor at the Institute.

I can never forget James D. ("Buddy") Givens and Carroll S. Yaws, who deserve the gratitude of all who value the rule of law and honest government in Galveston County. They were the citizen investigators whose undercover work was crucial to the injunctions against the gambling houses, illegal saloons, and houses of prostitution in Galveston County 50 years ago. The two men, who worked in the refineries by day, put themselves and their families at great risk for no personal gain. Sadly, both died within a few years of the crackdown.

Thanks also to Virginia Messer of Eakin Press for making the book a reality and to my neurosurgeon, Dr. Joel Patterson of the University of Texas Medical Branch, for keeping me alive long enough to finish it.

But most of all, thanks to Connie for sharing the journey.

JAMES P. SIMPSON
April 2007

The Early Years

Jim Simpson (right) with big brother Bob in Copperas Cove about 1927.

What's in a Name?

Six siblings preceded me into this world. Dick, Marvel, Joe, Lynn, Jimmy Alene, and Bob were delivered without the assistance of a physician between the years 1909 and 1921. When I arrived my mother had a doctor present at birth for the first time. The family had not, however, progressed to the point that my birth would occur in a hospital. I was born in my parents' bedroom in our home in Corpus Christi, Texas. The year was 1923.

From that moment forward, I naively thought my true name was Jack Simpson. That's what my family called me, and I had no reason to question it.

In the 1930s, the U.S. Army operated a program known as Citizens Military Training Camp. The program provided for young men 17 years of age or older to enroll in a series of four successive summer sessions of 30 days each. Upon completion of the four summers of training, the CMTC cadet would be commissioned as a 2nd lieutenant in the Army Reserve in either infantry or field artillery. I had to lie about my age, because I was only 16 when I enrolled in 1940 as an infantry cadet under my presumed name of Jack Simpson.

I wanted to go to camp to escape the doldrums of Copperas Cove, where my family lived at the time. Copperas Cove had few sources of recreation. Going swimming in Blue Hole, a recreational spot on House Creek, was the most there was to offer. In addition, I knew from my grasp of current events that America was going to be involved in the war in coming months, and it would be useful to have some preparation in advance of regular military service.

The Citizens Military Training Camp got young men off the street and helped out families during the Depression by virtue of feeding a family member for a few weeks. During these years, many children were malnourished. For example, I only weighed 109 pounds when I reported for my physical exam. To qualify for the program, you had to weigh at least 110 pounds. I appealed to the doctor administering my physical exam, and he agreed to give me an extra pound and list me at 110. Three of us from Copperas Cove volunteered—my brother Bob, my friend Roy Cooper, and me. We reported to Camp Bullis, which was part of Fort Sam Houston in San Antonio, where we lived in a six-man pyramidal tent.

As my training advanced and we prepared to go on maneuvers, I found that my gear—a backpack, Springfield 30.06 rifle, web belt with canteen, either a pick or a shovel, and a half-shelter—weighed approximately 110 pounds. I was never sure if that's how the Army arrived at a minimum weight for a cadet or not. I enjoyed the camp, but it would be my last, because the CMTC was discontinued by the summer of 1941 in order to direct the resources to the preparation for war.

By December of that year, my brother Bob had enlisted in the Marine Corps and was stationed at Pearl Harbor. He was there on December 7, 1941, when the Japanese attacked. This sneak attack and its terrible casualties embittered me, and although I had not finished high school, I sought to volunteer for military service immediately. Because I was under age 21, I could not enlist without the permission of my parents. But my mother, who had great respect for the value of an education, refused to consent until I graduated from high school.

Shortly after Pearl Harbor, the Army eliminated the prerequisite of two years of college study for admission to the aviation cadet program. Instead, one could be admitted if he took an exam and demonstrated proficiency equal to two years of college. During the spring of 1942, my teachers in Copperas Cove helped me study for this test, which was administered in San Antonio. The test covered some subjects I had never studied, such as chemistry and physics. Nevertheless, I passed the written test, the physical exam, and the other requirements for flight training and was to be sworn in as an aviation cadet.

The Air Corps required proof of my age. I knew the process for getting a certified copy of my birth certificate. I composed a letter to the county clerk of Nueces County, where I was born, explaining that my parents were James Polk Simpson and Eva Curtis Simpson, and that I had made my debut into this world on September 27, 1923. In short order, the district clerk's office sent me a letter stating they had no record of the birth of a Jack Simpson, but they did show the birth of a child named Giles Simpson of the same parents and on the same date as I had alleged. Giles? I didn't know any Giles Simpson.

It occurred to me that the Bureau of Vital Statistics in Austin might have recorded the event of my birth. A letter to this bureau brought back the report that they did show the birth of James P. Simpson, Jr., of the same parents and same date of birth. Apparently, this was the name my parents intended for me. Rumor had it that the doctor presiding at the time of my birth, Dr. Giles, had something of a drinking problem. It was said that if the good doctor could not recall the name a certain mother coveted for her child he would generously give the child his name. Thus, the birth certificate indicating that I bore the name of Giles Simpson. Of course, I have no personal knowl-

Summer soldier Jim, age 16, attending Citizens Military Training Camp at Ft. Sam Houston, San Antonio, in 1940.

edge of the doctor's condition at the time of my birth. Whatever the cause, I was faced with a dilemma: Should I claim to be Giles Simpson, James P. Simpson, Jr., Jack Simpson, or some other alias? I elected to choose the name of my father, James P. Simpson, and have borne that name into my years as an octogenarian. Once I became an adult, however, I chose not to affix "Jr." to my name. And to most people, I'm simply "Jim."

How, the reader might ask, did I end up bearing the name of James P. Simpson, Jr., in the first place? You must understand the nature of my sainted mother. She was the poster girl for permissive mothers. My mother had resisted naming my three older brothers after my father. But by the time I arrived, she resolved to name her next male offspring, James Polk Simpson, Jr. The only problem was that she had not consulted my older brothers and sisters. Upon hearing her decision, they pitched a fit. When my mother asked them what they wished to name the baby, they all settled on "Jack." No great quarrel about this, but it does occur to me that my family might have informed me of my true identity and of the circumstances of my name. Little harm, if any, ensued as I progressed from cotton picker to wood cutter to soldier to university student. On September 16, 1950, I was sworn in as a member of the State Bar of Texas as James P. Simpson.

All in all, I must say it has been a good life, whatever name I have borne.

Too Poor to Paint

In the bleak days of the Great Depression of the 1930s my parents struggled to raise a family of eight children, although my two eldest siblings had already left home by the time the Depression arrived in earnest. More than a fourth of all able-bodied men in America were unemployed, and many families existed at the poverty level, which is to say, the starvation level. Too many households were like our own—"too poor to paint, too proud to whitewash." This expression was a holdover from before the Depression, when a whitewashed home bore the stigma that the owner was too impoverished to afford paint. Many young people today have never seen whitewash, a watery form of paint which is both less expensive and less effective than paint.

Living next to us in our very modest neighborhood was a family even more destitute than we were. This family consisted of Mr. and Mrs. Clyde McVey and their eight children.

Previously my father had owned a small country weekly newspaper on the Gulf Coast of Texas but it was swept away by the tropical hurricane of 1919, although he would later start another newspaper in Copperas Cove. He was now unemployed most of the year. Despite all these handicaps, my mother sought to set a table for her brood. We had a garden which provided various vegetables. A milk cow provided enough milk for the family.

Franklin D, Roosevelt was elected President in 1932, promising "a new deal for America." He spoke of a nation that was "ill clad, ill housed and ill fed." The McVeys and the Simpsons fit this description. Young Clyde McVey and I were contemporaries. Clyde often found it convenient to be visiting our home at mealtime, and my mother did not have the heart to send him home hungry. His feet were to be found under our table several times a week. Ultimately, Clyde realized the inequity of this arrangement. One day he said to my mother, "Mrs. Simpson, I done et offn you folks, now I want little Jack to come home and eat offn us." A prospect that I did not look forward to. The McVeys were not only poor, but they suffered from tuberculosis and their respect for hygiene was not unduly fastidious. So I was not eager to sup at their table. Of course, I joined Clyde at his family's table to be polite.

Even Clyde's language betrayed the misery of those days. "I done et offn you folks, now I want little Jack to come home and eat offn us." President Roosevelt was concerned with social afflictions that were undermining the strength of America. Meanwhile, the conservatives of the day insisted that it was not the business of government to deal with malnutrition, hunger, and disease.

8   Flak Bait

Jim (center) with his catch from deep sea fishing in Port Aransas with two boyhood friends. They had gone fishing with older brother Dick and Captain Don Farley, who had taken President Franklin D. Roosevelt fishing the previous week.

Tuberculosis was a disease of poverty. It flourished where poor living conditions and poor nutrition existed. Its onslaught transformed the McVeys and many other families into gaunt, sickly figures. The Constitution guarantees us the right to "life, liberty, and the pursuit of happiness." Surely the eradication of poverty and disease is a worthy endeavor for our government. Growing up in such poverty caused me to be concerned about the health and safety of others, an interest that later played an important influence in my law practice. I'm sure it also played a significant role in my liberal political orientation. To this day, I feel very grateful to have escaped the ravages of poverty and tuberculosis.

In one of life's ironies, in 1970 I built a large comfortable redbrick home on several acres situated on Dickinson Bayou in Galveston County, Texas. The architect recommended whitewashing the brick exterior and then having the painters remove part of the finish in the interest of giving the house an aged appearance. No longer "too proud to whitewash," I was delighted to concur.

Cheaper by the Half Dozen

My mother, whose full maiden name was Eva Curtis Green, took pride in being Irish, and she poked fun at my father for being of Scottish descent. While she could be abrasive, she was very sensitive about anyone saying something against her blood kin. She defended her family above all.

For example, her younger brother, Bob Green, ran a touring car back in the 1930s in Cisco, Texas. Touring cars might be considered the precursor of taxicabs, although taxicabs probably do not ply the streets of Cisco even today. On one occasion, two oilmen had hired Bob Green to drive them around the oil fields for a couple of days. At the end of their travels, they refused to pay Bob for his services. Upon hearing this, my mother asked Bob where the oilmen were.

"Down at the oil prospector's office," he replied.

My mother went down to the office and started beating the two men with her umbrella. She was so combative that the police were called, and they arrested my mother.

When she went before the municipal judge, he asked her why she got involved in the dispute.

"That's my baby brother!" she exclaimed, "And these men are trying to cheat him!" I don't know if she was successful in collecting Bob's fee, but she definitely made an impression on the two oilmen.

People thought twice before crossing Eva Curtis Green. My mother's confrontational manner served her well when she was forced to shop for her large family.

A general once observed that, "War is hell." I believe that my mother could have testified that poverty is also hell. During the Depression, with six of her eight children still under her roof, she endeavored to house, feed, and clothe the family in spite of the fact that my father was unemployed most of the time. So in those difficult days a mother had to carefully utilize every resource to the fullest. Money had virtually ceased to be a medium of exchange. One year, with winter fast approaching — bringing with it rain, sleet, snow, and viciously cold weather — my mother planned a shopping trip.

Mother had saved her small change for several weeks, hoping to build up a fund from which she could put shoes on the feet of her children. When finally she felt she might have enough money, she gathered us all together, and we set out on foot to downtown Waco. There were two major department stores in Waco in the 1930s—Sanger-Harris and Goldstein-Migel. Although we gave no hint of affluence, it must have been heartening for the salesman to greet a mother with six offspring in obvious need of footwear.

"Good morning, Mrs. Simpson. How nice to see you and these beautiful children this morning. How may I help you?"

To which my mother replied, "Don't go sweet talking me. I want to know if you really want our trade."

She knew full well he wanted our trade, and she knew the

old belief that a good first sale of the day might be a precursor to a great day of retail trade. My mother was mentally prepared to be hard to deal with and intent on driving a hard bargain.

Even as a five-year-old lad, I felt sorry for the poor sales clerk. He hauled out practically every shoe in the house in a valiant effort to fit six children at a price that would not invoke the wrath of my precious mother. All the while she was reminding the salesman of the imperative need to stay within the bounds of her budget.

Finally he succeeded in finding a pair for each child and was putting a pencil to his pad as my mother once more admonished, "You had better get right with me and these children because you are not the only pebble on the beach!" She was prepared to be bitter no matter what price the salesman quoted. Finally, he stated he could have us all in shoes for a total of $5.95, slightly less than one dollar per child.

My mother promptly grabbed my hand and, almost jerking my arm out of its socket, she exclaimed, "Let's get out of here, Little Jack. They don't want none of our business."

She then marched us all to the door as the salesman protested, "Come back here, Mrs. Simpson. I'll get right with you."

"Well, you had better, because Goldstein-Migel is having a sale just down the street," my mother threatened.

Mother came to terms with the salesman, and six kids became the proud owners of new shoes. I have often wondered what profit, if any, remained for the poor salesman.

I suppose the salesman felt much as I did several decades later when as a lawyer, I had an injury case that turned out to be weaker than I anticipated. Despite the fact that I had invested much time in preparing the case, as the trial date approached, I knew it was not worth spending a week at the courthouse.

My opposing counsel, Tom Weatherly, a senior attorney at Vinson & Elkins in Houston, had offered a small settlement. My case had turned out to be not only of dubious value, but also none too appealing to a jury. An inauspicious combination.

Nevertheless, I tried to get Tom to increase the settlement offer. He replied in a silky voice, "Ah, Jimmy, you don't want any of the cheese. You just want out of the trap."

I'm sure the shoe salesman felt the same way after serving my mother. He'd long since given up on the cheese, and he just wanted out of the trap.

Momma Knows

Eva Curtis Green was lawfully wed to my loving father in 1905, and together they brought forth eight children. To say that my mother was a bit unorthodox would be a mastery of understatement. She verily believed that each and all of her children were perfect. She died at age 87, never having discovered the slightest defect in any of her children. She did not believe in spanking. Rather, she resorted to scaring the living daylights out of her children. She teased us unmercifully, but we always knew she loved the water we walked on. Even as a child, I remember reflecting that there was bound to be error in her totally unquestioning love for us. Her teasing never took a malicious note. Rather, it was a loving type of interaction.

She had four daughters. I recall her telling each of them at various times, "Pat (or Lynn, or Marvel), don't go gettin' married. Just be an old maid, and raise your kids to suit yourself." I should point out that momma was an agnostic, and wasn't overly impressed by organized religion.

If I inquired of her on certain topics, she would usually say, "Youngun, I don't understand all I know about that." Or, she might say, "I can't tell you that, youngun, because if I did, you would know as much as I know."

In my earliest years, I aspired to have spending money by working in the cotton fields near our home. The pay was 40 cents per hundred pounds, which on a good day, would translate to about half a dollar. Each cotton season, mother would dispatch my father and me to the general store, where we would buy enough cotton ducking material to make cotton sacks for those children who would be picking cotton that year. Once the cotton sack was made, and a strap affixed to it, I was in business. She would throw the new cotton sack at me, and say "here, youngun, I'm gonna give you half of what you make."

Needless to say, neither she nor I earned enough money for retirement. I did learn one thing indelibly, however, and that was that I did not want to spend my life as a cotton picker. My siblings didn't fare much better.

My mother had an undying pride in our slightest accomplishments. If I brought home from the county meet a blue ribbon in spelling or declamation, I was singled out for high praise by my mother. When I returned from the war in Europe, she would tell you with a straight face that I was the major reason for the war terminating in favor of the Allies, and she left little doubt about that. She would acknowledge that General Eisenhower had played some slight role in that conflict, but the true hero of the war was her baby boy. On my return, she announced to one and all that I would be shortly leaving to go to the University of Texas to obtain a law degree and a law license.

Years later, when I had moved both her and my father to Texas City to be near me in their later years, she would meet someone on the street and immediately inquire, "Do you know my son, Jack? He's a big lawyer here in town." Daniel Webster had nothing on me, and Clarence Darrow, the famed criminal defense lawyer, was a mere errand boy for others.

I took her and my father with me when I went to argue before the United States Court of Appeals. She listened attentively as I presented oral argument to the court, imploring the court to grant relief to my deserving client. Seven other cases were argued that same morning, meaning that a minimum of 14 very able lawyers had argued before the court. As we emerged from the courtroom with my mother on my arm, she looked up at me and said, "You were the best." She said this with such fervor that there was no questioning her judgment. We used to say about mother that she may not always be right, but she was never in doubt.

I didn't take to heart her every pronouncement, but I loved her more than any child loved a mother.

The Copperas Cove Crony

For several years during the 1920s my father, James Polk Simpson, was the owner, publisher, editor, and sole employee of a weekly publication known as *The Copperas Cove Crony*. The nature of the *Crony* was best summed up by the motto that appeared below the masthead every Thursday: "The Only Newspaper in the World That Gives a Damn About Copperas Cove."

The Crony relied for its income largely on what was then known as job printing—individual orders of advertisements and handbills paid for by merchants and other small businesses.

Studying ancient copies of *The Crony*, as I did a few years ago, revealed that my father was a man of diverse interests. He appeared to be a product of the times in which he lived and worked. He took note of the significant political happenings and reported on the events of the day. *The Crony* was never highly successful as a business enterprise. Indeed, both the *Crony* and our family skirted the edge of bankruptcy most of the time.

It was said that folks didn't read the *Crony* to find out what had happened. In such a small community, they knew what happened. They read the *Crony* to see who got caught.

Several theories have been advanced regarding the ultimate collapse of *The Crony*. The most likely version was that one week the editor dispatched a young photographer to take a photo of an ancient building in town that was scheduled for demolition, a building as old as the Alamo itself and even more decrepit. My father had already written the caption to go under the picture of the old building.

But the best laid plans can go awry, and this was certainly one example. Daddy was about to go to press when a youngster dashed into the pressroom shouting, "Hold the presses! The wife of the mayor has just died." The wife of the mayor, whatever other admirable qualities she might possess, was not noted for either beauty or intellect. Additionally, she was not very popular. My father removed the picture of the ancient edifice and substituted in its place a picture of the mayor's late wife. The only problem was that he failed to change the caption.

Five hundred copies of *The Crony* went forth with the mayor's wife pictured on page one above this caption: "Old Eyesore Gone at Last."

It might be argued that the newspaper was never destined to succeed, but there's no doubt that the demise of the mayor's wife and the ensuing blunder contributed to the failure of *The Copperas Cove Crony*.

The Saga of the Relief Shirts

During the Depression, when a family became impoverished and unable to support its members, the father sought to go "on relief." In 1933, this federal program provided employment for men to work on road projects for a paycheck of $10 per week. This might seem to be a pitiful amount, but when a family had known unemployment for weeks on end, it was regarded as manna from heaven. In addition, the relief program made family members eligible for government-issued clothing.

A staple among the clothing offered was the "relief shirt." It was light weight and made of blue chambray cloth. The shirts were readily identifiable, and wearing such a shirt announced to all that the family was in desperate financial straits. Some children were too embarrassed to wear relief shirts and preferred to wear their own threadbare rags. For me, at age 10, the utility of the shirt outweighed the stigma that it bore.

One day at school while I was wearing a relief shirt, a schoolmate of mine who came from an affluent family held me up to ridicule by saying to one and all in a loud voice, "Look at little Jackie Simpson wearing one of them there relief shirts." Although he was larger than I was, I tore into him in a blind rage and did considerable harm to the appearance of his face. In other words, I beat the hell out of him. This discouraged other students from making fun of the less fortunate children whose families were struggling with poverty.

My brother and I were about the same age and the same size. We had two cousins about our age. Their mother owned a small newspaper, *The Orange Leader*, which thrived even in Depression days. No relief shirts for them. Instead their clothes bore the label of Neiman Marcus of Dallas. Pride did not keep us from receiving their hand-me-down clothes. They attended elite summer camps, while my brother and I went to military camp serving alongside regular Army soldiers of the famous Second Infantry Division. We kept as many clothes from our short military experience as we could. My cousins were nice guys, and we bore them no ill will despite our difficult circumstances. My siblings and I learned firsthand the sad effects of poverty and hard times.

The Texas Centennial

In the summer of 1936 the State of Texas celebrated her centennial. In recognition of a century of independence from Mexico, this occasion was accompanied by a great deal of hoopla and hype. Advertisers and publicists sought to tap into the rich vein of Texas pride. Billboards everywhere urged folks to go to Dallas, the major site of the Centennial. I was then 12 years of age and my brother Bob was 14. We were caught up in the frenzy of celebrating the birth of Texas and 100 years of history. Newspapers were filled with descriptions of the many exhibits to be enjoyed. Bob and I were unlikely visitors but we were swept up in all the promotions that proclaimed the joy of learning more about Texas history.

We had never been to Dallas, then the largest city in Texas, some 100 miles north of our home in Copperas Cove. The Depression was well under way, and unemployment was rampant. Our family could scarcely afford a trip to Big D. But Bob and I were determined. We implored our father to take us to Dallas without success. We lobbied our Dad night and day, pointing out to him the many advantages that would accrue from such a trip. Dad pointed out the impossibility of our dream. We agreed that we would pick cotton at 40 cents per hundred pounds from July 1st to August 20 and would devote all of our earnings to the trip.

Cy Clayton lived next door and was privy to our pestering of my father to make the trip. Cy was a World War I veteran who had been gassed by the Germans in the trenches in France, leaving him with a terrible pulmonary disease. He spoke haltingly in a high-pitched voice.

One day during the lobbying, Cy had heard all of our many arguments and he said to my father, "Polky, why don't you take them there boys to that there sentimental?" (My father's middle name was Polk, as is mine.) Cy's fervent plea for the "sentimental" closed the sale. Daddy finally agreed, and preparations began for the trip.

We would go in Dad's 1928 Model A Ford. We anticipated that our earnings would buy the gas and oil and provide for a minimum of two night's lodging.

The day we were to leave, we awoke at four o'clock in the morning, and after a hasty breakfast, we got under way. We had to watch every penny because we needed to pay for gas, oil, food, admission fees, and other costs. I'll always remember driving through towns such as Belton, Temple, Waco, Waxahachie, and ultimately into Dallas. Our entry into Big D was heralded by the famous Mobil Oil Company sign, a red neon flying horse, which towered over the big bridge leading into downtown. What a thrill this was for two youngsters whose greatest experience had been a 30 mile trip to Gatesville, our county seat.

The Centennial was held at Fair Park, home of the Texas State Fair. We had no reservations for the night, because the cost of a long distance phone call would have depleted our travel budget. Luckily we found an old rundown hotel right across the street from Fair Park where for one dollar a night we found lodging in a single room lit by a light bulb hanging from the ceiling. Bathroom facilities were just down the hall.

We were too keyed up at the prospect of what we were to see and learn to even be aware of our meager accommodations. In spite of being weary from the journey in an open car, we had great trouble falling asleep. We asked our Daddy a thousand questions, and although he had the patience of Job, we must have driven him crazy.

The next morning we went across the street to the Centennial, and we were shocked at the admission price charged for many exhibits. We sought out all of the free exhibits and then carefully parsed the other exhibits with a keen eye to our modest funds. We were thrilled to go to the Eddie Rickenbacker exhibit. Captain Rickenbacker was the Ace of Aces, having shot down 28 German aircraft in the First War. We studied every photograph and examined every artifact. There was no admission charge, but the gimmick was that they tried to shake down visitors at the exit. We finally struck a bargain by which we paid the exhibit 10 cents per boy and 20 cents for my father.

An exhibit we greatly wanted to see was known as the Cavalcade of America, which depicted the discovery, expansion, and the growth of America from the time of Columbus to the present. We were heartbroken to find the cost of this exhibit was one dollar each, far exceeding our resources. However, many major corporations had exhibits which were free and which touted the advances and contributions of the exhibitor. For lunch we stopped at a hot dog stand, where a hot dog and a Coke cost 15 cents.

The people running the Centennial were very kind, and I remember one employee who let us in for free, overlooking the admission charge.

As the day wore on, we wore out. My father was greatly relieved when Bob and I agreed we would get up early the next morning and drive back to Copperas Cove. We had been too long at the fair but it was worth every effort and every last penny. We reported to Cy Clayton that the Texas Sentimental had been well worth the cost of admission.

County Meet

Each spring in Coryell County there came an event of some magnitude in our community. It was known as "county meet" and was the stepchild of the famous Roy Bedichek, the author and perhaps the original Texas environmentalist. He was later to publish the book *Adventures with a Texas Naturalist*, which remains a highly influential work and a part of the Texas literary canon.

For decades, Bedichek championed the county meet through his leadership of the University Interscholastic League, commonly called UIL, the organizing body of athletic and academic competition in the public schools in Texas. He was director of UIL, which was established by the University of Texas, for 26 years.

Each rural school district, including Copperas Cove, sent a delegation to the county seat, in our case, the town of Gatesville. The meet would include various track and field events, as well as academic competitions in spelling, declamation, mathematics, and other subjects. I competed in spelling and declamation and often brought home the blue ribbon in those events.

How well I recall memorizing Lincoln's Gettysberg Address

and John McCrae's poem: "In Flanders fields the poppies blow, between the crosses row on row..."

These events represented about all the cultural enrichment that could be obtained around Copperas Cove in those days of the Great Depression. Interestingly enough, Roy Bedichek had grown to manhood just a few miles away at Eddy, Texas, where his parents jointly managed an institution of learning known as Bedichek Academy.

I was not universally acclaimed as an athlete in any sport but I became interested in tennis after discovering a book by then-national champion Don Budge, appropriately entitled *How to Play Tennis*. The book instructed me to grasp a tennis racket in the same manner as one would shake hands. Then I followed the book's advice on how to slice, to volley, and to hit a backhand shot.

The book also described the dimensions of a tennis court. On the grounds of Copperas Cover High School, I drew up a court with a tape measure and wood stakes. To create the lines, I scored a groove in the dirt with a sharp stick and filled the groove with lime. When I finished, civilization had finally arrived in the form of Copperas Cove's first ever tennis court!

I mastered the intricacies of tennis as best I could without an opponent. Then, once armed with my newly acquired skills, I sought about training a partner. This would enable the two of us to represent Copperas Cove High School in tennis at the county meet some 30 miles distant. I drafted my friend, Roy Cooper, as my tennis pupil. Once properly trained, he indeed became my doubles partner at the county meet, and I also played in the singles competition. I won the blue ribbon as county champion in singles. Roy and I did not do quite so well in doubles, but it was a fine experience for both of us nonetheless. I was later to play in intramural tennis competition at the University of Texas.

I was entirely self-taught, and while I never achieved much further acclaim as a tennis player, it gave me a great deal of pleasure and healthy exercise over the years.

Entrepreneurship

I spent most summers during the 1930s at a place called Station C, a company town near Utopia, Texas. Station C was owned and operated by Humble Pipeline Company, for whom my brother Dick worked. Dick was 14 years my senior and already married. In order to assure that I was welcome in his home, I was eager to cut the lawn, help with the housework, help care for my brother's young baby, and otherwise make myself useful. Station C was up in the Hill Country of Texas, about 45 miles north of Kerrville. For a teenage lad, it was virtually heaven on earth.

To make things complete, I enjoyed the friendship of a sidekick who was my age, Rip Martin. Together, we swam in the Medina and Sabinal rivers. We played tennis both night and day, and literally, we lived the life of Tom Sawyer and Huckleberry Finn.

Station C was the site of a booster station, which boosted pipeline pressure in lines that transported oil from the West Texas oilfields to the oil refineries on the Texas Gulf coast. Other than to increase pipeline pressure, the hamlet of Station C had no reason to exist.

Located on one of the high points in the Hill Country, the terrain of Station C possessed a rugged beauty, with rocky hills, clear rivers, and abundant deer, wild turkeys, and other game. Executives from the Humble Pipeline Company in Houston and Corpus Christi traveled to Station C in the fall to stay at the company's large ranch house and take advantage of the excellent deer hunting.

One day during my summer stay, my sidekick Rip and I discussed the fact that we should be doing something creative—perhaps finding a means of employment. In those years, there were no fast food places, no minimum wage laws, and scant little opportunity for enterprising young lads. In counsel with my older brother, Dick, we decided that Rip and I would go into business for ourselves. Many homes in the Hill Country had fireplaces, and hence there was always a need for firewood. We had a few dollars from our allowance, and we bought a crosscut saw for 50 cents. To clinch the deal, the owner of the saw threw in, for good measure, a single-bit axe. Now we were in business!

Rip and I discovered that a cord of wood would sell for four dollars. If we delivered the wood, the price was five dollars per cord. We set our own working hours, which we described as being from sun to sun, meaning from sunrise to sunset. The crosscut saw was manned by one of us at one end and the other at the other end. It was hard work, but it was good for our development as young men.

My hope was to sell enough cord wood to be able to buy my clothes and school supplies for the coming winter. This I did, and more. During one of the summers, I abandoned the saw and went to a military camp at Fort Sam Houston, San Antonio. I found that I was much better prepared for the physical rigors of military training than city boys who had never wielded an ax nor pulled a saw. When I joined the Army Air Corps in 1942, I soon realized that my wood cutting days were a real bonus to me. Military training was demanding, but I had not the slightest problem in passing the strenuous physical examinations.

A summer of woodcutting would yield 25 to 30 dollars. After buying a new winter jacket and some cotton khaki pants, I gave the remainder to my mother, who had a difficult time caring for six children. The lessons I learned about fending for myself and gaining independence were invaluable. I've often wished that somehow every lad growing up in America could have a profitable experience as a young entrepreneur.

The War

An Encounter in Los Angeles

Rarely have two brothers been so close as Bob Simpson and his baby brother. I was born September 27, 1923, while Bob preceded me in this world on December 17, 1921. Growing up together, many people thought of us as twins, although the resemblance was not striking. Together we had attended Citizen's Military Training Camp in the summer of 1940. It was rugged infantry training, and we were issued a 30.06 rifle, the Army's standard weapon of the First World War. Bob took military training with greater zest than I demonstrated. Once Bob concluded that World War II was drawing nigh, he decided to enlist right away. After we returned from military camp, he decided to join the U.S. Marine Corps. Our mother was not anxious to have him do so, but he was not to be denied. Finally, our mother and father agreed to sign the necessary papers for him to enlist in the fall of 1940. After boot camp at the Marine Corps center in San Diego, Bob was sent to guard the U.S. Naval Air Station at Kanoehe on Oahu. He was promoted in rank to private first class and soon thereafter to the rank of corporal.

Things were not the same without the company of brother Bob in Copperas Cove. I always regretted that our paternal grandmother was so obviously devoted to me and much less so to Bob. Fortunately this did not adversely affect my relationship with my brother. He had the patience of Job. Bob enjoyed the camaraderie of serving in the Marines, and he wanted me to follow him. With the approach of war, I became convinced I that should join the U.S. Army Air Corps and become a pilot. The pay was much better, and one would gain invaluable knowledge if one could succeed in the aviation cadet program.

In 1941, I was still living at home in Copperas Cove. On December 7th I had been climbing a small mountain near our home. When I returned about two o'clock in the afternoon that day, I found a delegation of relatives and friends gathered by the radio. I could sense something serious had occurred. My mother was seated in the living room and was quietly weeping. The radio had reported that the Japanese had carried out their infamous sneak attack on Pearl Harbor in Hawaii. Communication was slow, and it was not known whether my brother Bob had survived. As news of the attack was being broadcast, the U.S. Naval Air Station at Kaneohe, about 15 miles from the Naval installation at Pearl Harbor, was frequently mentioned. There was unbearable anxiety in our small living room as we awaited news of Bob.

My brothers tried to place a telephone call to Bob but their efforts were to no avail. A long, slow week passed before we learned that Bob had escaped injury on December 7th.

I was a senior in high school and not required at that time to register for the draft. I wanted to immediately enlist on hearing of the devastation wrought by the Japanese. My mother insisted that I graduate from high school before joining the military, and at my age, I could not enlist without the signature of my parents. I completed high school that spring, and on June 5, 1942, I was sworn in as an aviation cadet. I was called to active service on November 11, 1942, and was immediately sent to Santa Ana, California, for flight training.

Meanwhile, Bob returned from Hawaii and was stationed at the Marine Corps station at San Diego, some 90 miles south of Santa Ana. We corresponded and resolved to see each other at the earliest possible opportunity. It had now been two years since he had left home, the longest span of time we had ever been apart. We found it difficult for both of us to get a three-day pass at the same time. Finally, I was allowed a weekend pass, but I did not have time to notify Bob in advance so that that we might meet.

At Santa Ana I boarded the single gauge railway passenger train, which carried me to the station at Los Angeles, where I was still about 100 miles north of San Diego. Train stations in those days were crowded with service men and women from all of the branches. I knew the chances of my running into my brother were slim to none. It would have been like finding a needle in a haystack. Getting off the train in Los Angeles I dared to speculate on the possibility I might encounter Bob on the streets

Jim as an aviation cadet on a two-day pass in Los Angeles, 1942.

of Los Angeles. It is hard to imagine the elation both of us felt when we ran right squarely into each other on the sidewalk outside the train station.

I saw this tall handsome Marine approaching me and was shocked upon recognizing my hero and brother Bob G. Simpson. We hugged and danced on the streets of Los Angeles and then went to find a place for lunch. We talked incessantly, trying to bring each other up to date on the happenings since our last time together.

Soon we found a place where we could have our picture taken together. Then we wrote a letter to our parents enclosing the picture, which appears in these pages. A few weeks later I received another weekend pass and journeyed to the Marine Corp station at San Diego, where I stayed overnight in the barracks where Bob lived. We still could hardly believe our paths had crossed.

Army Air Corps turret repair school in Indianapolis. Jim on the left with three fellow soldiers.

I had a few more weeks of pre-flight school, after which I was sent to a small pilot training school in Blythe, California. Bob could not find any way to get sufficient leave to go back to Copperas Cove, and I was likewise unable to interrupt my own training. We were not to meet again for two years. In November, 1945, Bob was honorably discharged and returned home. I had been released the previous July. Needless to say there was much celebration at our family home in Copperas Cove when once more Bob and I were reunited.

Lana Turner and Me in Palm Springs

In June 1943 my dearest friend was a fellow Texan, Roy Lee Campbell, who hailed from Kenedy, Texas. If there was any person in our flight class at Blythe, California who was more country and unsophisticated than I was, it was my friend Roy Lee. He was my age, 18, and he had a vivid imagination. Somehow he became convinced that if he and I could find our way to the desert resort of Palm Springs, California, many memorable adventures would ensue.Indeed, Roy Lee was confident that if he and I journeyed to Palm Springs for the weekend, by Saturday night one of us would be in the arms of Lana Turner and the other in the embrace of Rita Hayworth. With great earnestness, he presented a plan to me.

I was so absorbed in the possibility I might earn the wings of a pilot and Second Lieutenant in the U.S. Air Force that I had given Roy's plan no thought. Finally, after days of Roy Lee's insistence, I cross-examined him about the proposal. Not only was I skeptical about enjoying the company of two Hollywood stars, but we did not even have a means of transportation to Palm Springs. How could we get there? Roy's reply: "We'll hitchhike."

I pointed out that hitchhiking for an aviation cadet was an offense punishable by dismissal from the Aviation Cadet Program. I was listening to my fears while Roy Lee could only hear his hopes.

Finally, after a great deal of discussion, it was decided that the coming weekend would find us on the road to Palm Springs. We received a weekend pass and bummed a ride with a fellow cadet to the outskirts of Blythe, some 200 miles from Los Angeles. It was from the dusty shoulder of the highway that our journey would begin. According to Roy Lee, we were only hours away from being welcomed to the desert resort by Hollywood starlets.

We started hitchhiking along the desert highway, and soon I could see a U.S. Air Force staff car going the same direction as our destination. Was it really our lucky day? As the four-door 1940 Plymouth drew closer, I could see it bore a pennant on the bumper denoting the presence of a general officer. Suddenly my worst fears seemed imminent. A general would surely be aware of the regulation prohibiting hitchhiking as a means of transportation for future officers.

I told Roy we had now made a mess of things, that the general would soon arrange our court-martial, not to mention our dismissal from the flight program. I suggested to Roy that we should turn our back to oncoming traffic and pretend we indeed were not hitchhiking. We stepped lightly into the desert, trying to put as much real estate as possible between us and the general.

Our luck seemed to run out when we heard the screech of tires as the Plymouth came to a halt. Suddenly, we heard the sergeant driver bark out at us, "You men come over here! The general is offering you a ride in his car."

Blood ran cold in the veins of the two prospective pilots. The courageous streak in Roy Lee disappeared as he made his way to be seated on the front seat next to the sergeant driver, relegating me to the back seat next to the general.

I could sense that the general was more than a little fascinated by these two youngsters who looked like they were playing hooky from high school. He inquired as to the purpose of our trip to Palm Springs. I tried to explain that we were stationed nearby at a primary training field, and we simply had a weekend off to explore. I noted from his uniform he was not an Air Force officer but indeed was in the armored division, giving me some faint hope that he might be unfamiliar with the rules against hitchhiking. As I told him our primary mission out on the desert was learning to fly airplanes, I could sense a feeling of astonishment wash over the general as he bowed his head in dismay. As he looked at us closely—two skinny, uneducated, and inexperienced teenagers—I fancied I could hear him mutter to himself: "Oh dear God, have we come to this? Are we this desperate?"

Eventually, I spotted a road sign advising that Palm Springs was 60 miles down the road. My hopes were buoyed up at the thought we might yet avoid detection of our nefarious scheme.

The general could not have been kinder as he told us he would be parking the staff car at a motor pool, and we would be welcome to share a taxicab with him at his expense. The presence of a general officer created quite a stir at the motor pool, and the three of us were granted a wide berth. When we reached his destination, I thanked the general profusely. Giving him a snappy salute, I departed his company, relieved that I was not intercepted by the military police and court-martialed.

However, with regard to the weekend's primary mission, I must confess that neither Roy Lee nor I were destined to meet Lana Turner during our visit to Palm Springs. All's well that ends well.

One a Day in Tampa Bay

The bonds that are forged in the crucible of war are probably the strongest bond known to mankind. That was certainly true for me and remains so now more than 60 years later.

It fell my lot to serve in one of the most decorated groups of its size in the history of the Second World War. Having little aptitude for landing airplanes during pilot training, I was assigned to a B-17 bomber ground crew before advancing to the position of navigator and bombardier on a crew of the B-26 medium bomber built by Martin in Baltimore, Maryland. The B-26 had an inauspicious beginning when early test flights were marked with numerous fatal accidents. The bomber became known variously as the *Widow Maker*, the *Flying Prostitute*, and other less fetching names.

Many authorities originally believed the aircraft was not air worthy. Some even said it was not even aerodynamically sound. It became so unsafe that it became the subject of an investigation by then-Senator Harry Truman's War Preparedness Committee. During a 30-day testing period, 30 bombers were lost as a result of power failure on takeoff. The path of an aircraft taking off from MacDill Field, where the planes were tested, extended out over Tampa Bay. Often, as a result of insufficient power, the bomber and its six crew members ended up in Davy Jones' locker. Suffice it to say, new crew members greeted their assignment to the B-26 with much trepidation.

The Truman Committee urged that the miscreant bomber be junked and be replaced by the B-25 and the A-20, aircraft that did not have the same unsavory reputation. History was to show it was fortunate that the Truman Committee recommendation was not followed. Instead, a plan was conceived to increase the wingspan of the B-26, and thus increase lift and stability. This and other changes made the bomber viable, and it was committed to combat over German-occupied terrain in Europe in April 1942, shortly after Pearl Harbor.

While in Florida, I met some interesting characters, including Bill Pehr from Denver. Bill became a dear friend and would remain so throughout the war. At one point, Bill was just a few days away from graduating as a rated pilot. He had all the requisites for becoming a great pilot, except for the fact that he had a bad temper. One day while Bill was at the controls, an instructor pilot chastised him severely, and Bill lost his temper. When he brought the training plane back to earth, he continued to exacerbate the situation by continuing to quarrel with the instructor, whereupon he was washed out of the pilot training program.

This did not improve his outlook on life, because like me, he was relegated to ground service. Prior to our service in a B-26 squadron, we were both members of a B-17 squadron at MacDill Field. Bill and I were placed in the armament section, maintaining machine guns, bomb racks, gun turrets, and the like. To us, the work was a crushing bore. Bill pointed out to me, however, that our job had one saving grace, and that was that you were fairly assured of dying of old age, not from combat with the enemy. I reasoned that I would rather risk being killed than to suffer the certainty of boredom. I told Bill we should both ask to be sent to aerial gunnery school.

Bill was a reluctant dragon. Although he resisted, he ended up joining me in making a request to the squadron adjutant that we be transferred into the flight echelon. The next day, we were notified that we were to be sent to Fort Myers for gunnery training. Upon graduation into a combat crew, we received a 10 day leave, after which we were ordered to report to a replacement training unit at Barksdale Field, Louisiana. Here, the various crew members, pilot, co-pilot, bombardier, top turret gunner, and tail gunner, were formed into crews for further training. Classified as air combat crews, we were exempt from such tasks as guard duty and kitchen police. We were paid 50 percent extra as flying pay. All in all, life was much improved after leaving the B-17 squadron and joining the air crew in a B-26 squadron. There was more excitement, coupled with more danger.

Bill and I went on to join a great unit known as 451st Bombardment Squadron. Later in England, we would discover that boredom was rarely a problem in our squadron.

While I was in aerial gunner school at Fort Myers, I met one of the most interesting and colorful characters I was ever to meet. His name was Roland. Unlike me, who hailed from small town Texas, Roland spoke with an accent. It was pure Bronx. Roland had grown up in eastern New York State. He was a

34   **Flak Bait**

Weekend pass from Barksdale Field, Louisiana, 1944. From the left, Joe Simpson (Jim's older brother), Jim, Roy Cooper, and Louis Dewald. Cooper was Jim's high school tennis partner, and Dewald was then a Naval ROTC student at the University of Texas.

Louis Dewald, Jim, and Roy Cooper, 1944.

bright, earnest fellow, very cordial, and of unfailing good humor. But he was not much of a marksman. Indeed, he couldn't hit the floor with his hat.

We were introduced to aerial gunnery through skeet shooting. Clay pigeons, or disks, were launched into the air as targets and we were required to shoot them with a shotgun. Usually, in a morning of shooting, each gunnery candidate would fire on 25 clay birds. To break 18 out of the 25 was an acceptable score. The exercise taught us how to lead a moving target in the air. Fortunately, for me, I had grown up in central Texas, where I learned to shoot a shotgun, and it was not unusual for me to break 23 out of 25. All this was good practice for learning to defend against attacking German ME-109 fighters.

Roland and I compared scores at the end of each day of shooting. Unfortunately, Roland could not hit a bull in the ass with a bass fiddle. He announced one day that he destroyed eight out of 25 clay birds. When I told him I had broken 25 straight, his usual good temper did not prevail. Roland exploded. "To hell with youse Texans. Youse have to shoot. If you don't shoot, then youse don't eat!"

He was one of the guys from the big cities who genuinely believed that we Texans had to rise each morning and go forth to kill some unsuspecting creature in order to put meat on the table. Roland's command of the English language left something to be desired. He was a great guy, and I was very fond of him.

"Youse Texans, youse have to shoot. If you don't shoot, then youse don't eat!"

Aboard the *Ile De France*

In Depression-ridden central Texas the mere thought of going to Europe aboard a famed luxury liner was absurd. Indeed, before the advent of the Second World War, the farthest I had ever traveled from my home town of Copperas Cove was

36   Flak Bait

to San Antonio, a distance of some 200 miles. As it turned out I earned a berth on the *Ile De France* sailing from New York City to Grenock, Scotland.

I was now a crew member on medium-range bombers. Six of us were to serve as a replacement crew for the air war over Nazi Germany. We had just completed air crew training at Barksdale Field in Shreveport, Louisiana. We journeyed by passenger train from Shreveport to Savannah, Georgia. Once there, we were outfitted with a shiny new B-26 bomber to be flown to England and assigned to the U.S. 9th Air Force.

We were not chosen to ferry the new plane to the European theater of operations. Instead, we were destined to go by way of a troop ship to Scotland. From Savannah we rode a troop train to Camp Kilmer, New Jersey, where we awaited our passage

Jim's crew at Barksdale Field, Louisiana, August 18, 1944. From the left, Tom Mattax, Little Rock; Ralph Goldstein, Houston; Stan Adelman, Westport, CT; Herschel Tyson, Greenville, NC; Jennings Van Flossen, San Francisco; and Jim Simpson.

across the Atlantic. We had no idea as to which ocean-going vessel we would travel on to Europe.

A separate troop train took us to New York along with a large number of infantry replacements, many of whom were glider pilots, paratroopers, and ground pounders. On arrival in New York harbor, we saw the famous and luxurious *Ile De France*. To our surprise, this was our means of transport.

Living accommodations aboard the liner were less than ideal. Red Cross girls were waiting shipside and provided each soldier coffee and donuts, a first aid kit, and a copy of the Holy Bible.

The rumor mill had advised us that it was wise to take a carton of Hershey's chocolate bars. As I was not a smoker, I had plenty of space in my musette bag (a small backpack) for carrying a number of chocolate bars. The same rumor mill asserted that chocolate could be traded in Europe for virtually any item a soldier might require.

Sleeping quarters aboard the vessel were claustrophobic. Six fold-up canvas cots made up the sleeping area within each of the old cabins. Two meals a day were served, and this turned out to be a blessing as each meal consisted of a heap of spam and steaming hot coffee—no sugar, no cream—and a piece of bread.

Boredom was rampant. In fact I was so bored that I fell prey to a group of soldiers and airmen engaged in shooting craps. I rapidly increased my $100 paycheck to $500, a greater sum than I had ever known. Then luck failed me. A card shark entered the game and took virtually all of my worldly possessions.

Before leaving Savannah we had been outfitted with new flying gear, including fleece-lined leather jackets, flight coveralls, and leather boots. All of this would become important as we were to discover that we often would be flying at an altitude that brought with it 20-degree-below-zero temperatures. All of these items and more were stored aboard ship away from the men. Again misfortune seemed to be our lot, as every ounce of this new flying gear was stolen. I could hardly believe that our own G.I.s would stoop to stealing from combat air crews the equipment they desperately needed to wage war.

I survived the journey across the Atlantic solely by resorting to the chocolate I had bought in New York. It was a daunting prospect to think that we would be required to fly in sub-zero temperature wearing nothing but our woolen clothing, deprived of the fleece-lined jackets and warm leather gloves necessary to face the enemy under vicious weather conditions.

A group of bagpipers met the ocean liner at Grenock, Scotland. As our troop train journeyed over land farther into England toward the Channel coast, we observed a squadron of B-17s returning from a bombing mission over Germany and noted that some of the planes were missing from the formation.

We stayed on the troop train until it reached the village of Stone, England. This was known as a repple depple, or more properly, as a replacement depot. From there we would be assigned to operational units that would be engaged in bombing Nazi-held terrain. We were informed that we would be required to fly 65 missions over enemy territory before earning our right back to the zone of the interior, which is what the United States was called in military parlance. Even with my poor command of math, I recognized instantly the odds were not good.

I counted myself fortunate to be assigned to one of the most famous and distinguished combat outfits in the European theater. This was the celebrated 322nd Bomb Group known as Colonel Nye's Annihilators.

The group had flown the very first medium bombing missions in Europe. One of its first missions took the group across the English Channel to bomb a railroad bridge that was important to the German war machine. Twelve bombers from the squadron went aloft that day in May of 1942, well before I joined the unit. On takeoff a malfunction was discovered in one of the bombers, and it had to turn back. The remaining 11 B-26s pressed on, but a mishap doomed the mission to failure. One pilot suffered a severe loss of power. In order to save his aircraft, he had to climb above the extremely low altitude at which the group was flying. The bombers were flying barely higher than the treetops to avert detection by German radar. By increasing his altitude, the pilot of the stricken plane betrayed the remaining aircraft. Just as they were making landfall on a French coast, German flak gunners opened up with a volley of accurate and heavy flak. Three bombers were shot out of the sky and fell into the deep blue.

Still, the force pressed on with the remaining eight bombers, but two more were lost to the heavy guns of a flak tower. The remaining bombers spotted the target and commenced their bomb run. Four additional bombers were lost during the bombing. Now, there were four bombers of the initial 12.

As the remaining bombers approached the English Channel, gunners from a German war ship cut them up, leaving none of the aircraft to return. All twelve of the original planes were lost.

It was said that the Alamo had no messenger of defeat. The same could be said of the 322nd Bomb Group on its debut mission over German-held terrain. We had no messenger of defeat, and a heavy pall hung over the crews back at the base. It was traditional for crew members not assigned to the day's mission to gather with ground personnel at the flight line to greet the returning bombers. On this day, Nye's Annihilators had no survivors to bear witness to defeat.

A feeling of doom set in across the air base, and for days it was impossible to shake the depression that settled upon the unit. It was then decided to abandon low level bombing and to commence bombing at medium altitude, which is to say, ten to twelve thousand feet.

As bombardier, my private office on the B-26 was narrowly circumscribed. The bombardier had the job of manning a single 50 caliber machine gun. He had to make the intervalometer setting. He had to make sure the electrical current was in place for the dropping of each bomb. But my main job was to watch the lead ship. And as soon as I saw the lead ship open his bomb bay door, I opened my bomb bay doors. When he dropped his bombs, I dropped mine. After which I pushed the salvo button. For the four minute interval along the bomb run the pilot positively had to hold the plane straight and level, no movement right or left, up or down, in order to get a good bombing pattern on the ground.

On one mission, I was intent on watching the lead ship to the exclusion of all else, when all of the sudden I became aware of the pulsating red fluid entering my cramped compartment. My immediate thought was that some poor devil had lost a leg. I just hoped it wasn't me. We were told that since we were at altitude where the temperature ran to 30 or 40 degrees below zero, we might lose a limb and not even be aware of it.

Finally the lead ship opened the bomb bay doors and I did the same. And two minutes later, his first bomb fell, and I pressed the lever for my bombs to fall. Only then did I dare to investigate the matter of the red fluid. I reached up with my hands to see if I still had two of everything. Two eyes, two ears, two arms, two legs, two balls—and found that the problem was that a burst of flak had pierced a container of hydraulic fluid, which gave the appearance of blood.

We understood that we had a job to do, and the job took precedence over all else, including taking an inventory of one's gonads.

☆ ☆ ☆

All soldiers forge bonds in the heat of battle that are strong and enduring. And sometimes those bonds were not limited to human beings.

For much of our time in Europe, there were few diversions and joys for the men of the 451st squadron. One diversion we had was the affection of three precious dogs, Moe, Mimi, and Reddog, all of whom belonged to Captain Myron Sterngold, a loveable guy and a great leader of men. Captain Sterngold's favorite was Reddog. They were so attached to each other, that Reddog seemed to know when Captain Sterngold was leading a flight over Nazi Germany. He seemed to know when the planes were returning, and he would go down on the flight line to greet the squadron on its return, at which time a love fest between the

The War **41**

Reddog and the Captain would ensue to the great delight of the other crew members.

Soon Reddog commenced flying missions with the Captain. He positioned himself between the pilot and co-pilot and ran

Jim and a canine friend in Beauvais, France, 1944. G.I. blankets hang out to dry in the background, and the wood pile of bomb wreckage is the primary source of heat.

the same risks all of us encountered. Like the rest of us he became flak happy as aerial combat takes its toll on mind and body. To one degree or another we all suffered post traumatic stress disorder. Reddog was the only dog so far as history records who received the air medal for flights over enemy terrain.

At the end of the war came another problem: how was the Captain going to get these dogs back to America? For they would die of loneliness if they were left behind never to see their constant companion Captain Sterngold. While awaiting a ship in South Hampton the Captain and the dogs were down on the docks where a U.S Navy destroyer lay at anchor. Captain Sterngold encountered a sailor from the destroyer and said to him, "Young man, how would you like to earn $100?"

Gleefully the young sailor agreed. The Captain took a $100 bill and tore it in half giving the sailor one half with the Captain's address in New York City. He was assured that upon delivery of the dogs at a certain address the other one half would await him. The two halves—and the 3 dogs and their captain—were reunited. The Captain's canine friends lived happily ever after until death of natural causes.

While Moe, Mimi, and Reddog returned to a jubilant homecoming, not all veterans were as fortunate.

The Second World War was hardly over when a fellow named Daniel Inouye, upon returning from the European Theater, went to a barbershop in San Francisco—only to be told, "We don't wait on Japs." When this occurred, on his uniform was to be found a Silver Star and a Purple Heart. He had fought for this country while both parents were in a U.S. concentration camp.

And in the closing days of the war a Texan named Felix Longoria volunteered to go on a dangerous mission in the Philippines. His remains were not recovered until 1948. Yet when his body was returned to his hometown of Three Rivers, Texas, the local funeral home would not allow use of the chapel because, quote, "the whites would not like it." Furthermore, his family was required to bury the soldier in the "Mexican" section of the local cemetery, which was separated from the "white" section by barbed wire. Then Sen. Lyndon B. Johnson intervened and Felix Longoria was given a full military burial in Arlington National Cemetery.

While these events occurred 60 years ago in distant lands, let us bear in mind that at this very moment we must consider whether the rights and protections we espouse and defend overseas are respected and protected here on our own soil.

It is easy enough for the summer soldier and the sunshine patriot to wave the flag. But can we—and do we—stand up when it is not popular to do so to defend Constitutional rights? I believe that we do not have to accept the erosion of basic human rights in order to defend our national security.

The Irony of War

A great irony of the war was that our squadron was the victim of its own advanced skills in precision bombing. When France was occupied by Germany in 1940, the Luftwaffe took over a small air base near Beauvais, France. History buffs may recall that the Bishop of Beauvais played a prominent role in the trial and execution of the legendary Joan of Arc.

The Germans had used the air base, referred to in military lingo as Beauvais-Tille, as a fighter-bomber base. Tille is a small town adjacent to Beauvais in which the base is actually located. From this base, the Luftwaffe launched their assault upon the Hurricanes and Spitfires of the British Royal Air Force.

Long before D-Day in 1945, our intelligence services had proclaimed that Beauvais-Tille was of great military significance. On several occasions, our medium bombers, while still in England, launched their attack on the small German air base. The base was quite well defended with 88-millimeter flak guns, 105 millimeter weapons, and a respectable showing of ME-109 and FW-190 fighters.

Jim in 1944 holding the tail section of a Messerschmitt ME-109 fighter found at Beauvais-Tille, which had previously served as a German Luftwaffe fighter base.

The Messerschmidt E-109 was the equal of the famous Fokkerwulf-190 German fighter bomber. Fierce air battles raged in the region, with considerable losses on each side.

American and Allied ground forces overran and seized Beauvais shortly after the invasion. It was important that our medium bombers find or build airdromes at locations suited to our medium altitude and medium range bombers. A big part of our work consisted of bombing the lines of communication and transportation that served the German forces. Severing the enemy's rail and highway connections neutralized much of the effectiveness of the German military in the area.

After the Axis powers lost more French terrain to the Allies, we soon ran out of strategically located bases. Landing sites that were too far from the bombing targets were not usable, and the targets kept moving east as the Allies advanced. The air base at Beauvais-Tille, which was known as a favorite of Herman Goering, chief of the Luftwaffe, seemed a perfect fit for our unit. But, we arrived in this area, known as the Ile de France, in the fall of 1944, just in time for one of the most severe winters in the history of the European continent. We needed to build a tent city for living space, refurbish the bombed out hangers, and re-work the runways. All of this turned out to be a greater task than originally thought. As we attempted to begin combat missions over Axis-held terrain, we discovered that our accurate bombing missions prior to the invasion had been too successful.

Early morning takeoffs from the runway often ended in tragedy, as quite frequently one or more of our bombers would crash through the icy runway into a bomb crater—a bomb crater created by one of the bombs our own planes had dropped on the airbase when it was in German hands. Ultimately, after a sudden thaw, it was decided that the runways at Beauvais were too perilous to launch combat missions from without major repairs. One hundred five holes were counted in the runway. But the harsh weather was now making all forms of outdoor activity very difficult. Something had to be done! Winter was once more proving to be our worst enemy.

Initially, 9th Air Force headquarters sought the help of the

U.S. Corps of Engineers, who studied the problem with great dispatch and skill. Then came their report: with a streak of good luck and some moderation of the harsh weather, the engineers hoped to have the runways repaired and our bombers in the skies within 60 days. When this news arrived in the small bombed out village of Tille, you could have cut the cold silence with a knife. And when the ground forces were informed of this dilemma, they were even more devastated. They urgently needed air support to proceed with the invasion.

Given these facts, what were the options open to the air forces, who desperately wanted to aid the struggling forces on the ground, where a terrible toll was being taken on men and machines?

There was little time for pondering. The group commander, Col. John Samuel, and our squadron commander, Lt. Col. Henry Newcomer—classmates at the U.S. Military Academy at West Point—moved with swift dispatch. All personnel, ground and air, officer and enlisted man, young and old, would report the next morning at 0600 hours. The commanders had located a quarry of hard rock and gravel 26 miles away and several heavy trucks. As the trucks began to roll, the air strip took on the appearance of a bee hive. Night and day the men worked relentlessly and with little complaint. We well knew every minute we could save would be translated into sparing the lives of our combat ground forces.

What a sight to behold it was! Here one could see a highly skilled navigator whose experience and knowledge made him indispensable in the execution of a combat mission. A severe injury to him could cripple our effort once we did get airborne. Or a sergeant whose greatest skill before the war was his ability to move a pigskin down the football field—now his strength and determination could turn the tide of battle.

Morale among the men remained high throughout the monumental task before us. We were working on the basis of what became known as the maximum effort. We worked as though our very lives depended on repairing the runways. Hot food was brought to the work site in order to maximize the daylight hours available to us. Finally, our task was completed. The desperately cold weather had held our bombers on the ground, but now, it appeared that we might once more take to the air.

Rather than requiring the 60 days that the Corps of Engineers estimated, the repairs were completed in six days. American ingenuity and tireless human effort had triumphed. Now if only the weather would cooperate.

A check with the alert list at squadron operations office revealed the name of my crew on the next day's mission. I went to bed by 9:00 P.M., so tired and sore that sleep came easily. It seemed like days later, although it was only a matter of a few hours, before we were awakened and alerted for the mission. We were to bomb a large concentration of enemy troops and materiel. Hurriedly, we jumped into our flying gear, complete with flak suits and protective clothing. A hot breakfast was served, and then we gathered at the briefing room for intense instructions on what to expect. The weather had broken clear and cold and it showed signs of remaining that way.

Soon the roar of 36 medium bombers could be heard throughout the countryside. The mission was quite successful, with minimum losses, although another group that immediately preceded us on the target lost 16 of its 36 bombers. We always understood that the price of freedom was not small.

☆ ☆ ☆

On November 9, 1944, our bomber squadron made a deep penetration into the Third Reich. Our aircraft was under the command of a remarkable pilot, Tom Mattax. Lieutenant Mattax was two years out of the cotton fields of Lone Oak, Arkansas. On this day we ranged deeper into enemy terrain than we ever had in the process of bombing the railroad yards at Koblenz, Germany. Soon the weather turned on us, buffeting the twin-engine bomber with great force and violence, causing us to consume fuel at much greater than normal rate. Our airplane could remain airborne for only about 5 hours, at the end of which time it had to be on the ground somewhere. An hour after leaving the

48 Flak Bait

target area, a red warning light on the instrument panel told the pilot he had a mere 15 minutes in which to land. The weather now was closing in and visibility was severely limited.

Frantically, all crew members searched for a landing spot. We saw an abandoned airdrome previously used by the German Luftwaffe but its runways were pocked with deep holes, each hole representing an allied bomb. No dice. We would merely have ground up in a crash, probably accompanied by fire. The pilot spotted a narrow roadway between two villages in a rural area. He got on the intercom advising the rest of us we were free to bail out or ride the bomber down with him. I looked down from about 3,000 feet. A snowstorm with minus 20 degree temperature raged below. I concluded that even if I survived the parachute jump I would surely freeze to death in the storm. All crew members elected to stay with the bomber.

The pilot then gave orders to assume crash landing positions. My greatest fear was the tendency of the B-26 to burn on crash landing thus becoming our own funeral pyre. The roadway was clogged with rural traffic, such as trucks, wagons, and other farm equipment. The traffic jam came quickly unclogged as the pilot lowered the massive tricycle landing gear. There were probably no atheists aboard that plane. The young pilot with great skill guided it to a safe landing on a road barely wide enough to accommodate the huge landing gear. Not even so much as a sprained ankle was suffered and we had landed within Allied lines.

We were greatly relieved to see friendly faces where we had half expected to be captured by the Germans and marched off to a prisoner of war camp. No one on the crew spoke French and in the crowd of onlookers who had gathered around our plane no one appeared to speak English. I was able to use my high school Spanish, which is similar to French, and we thereby learned we had landed some 20 miles from an American night fighter airbase.

The villagers provided a place for the night and the next morning an Army truck came from the airbase near Dijon. At the Dijon airbase we were treated like visiting royalty. Wine and champagne were brought forth and we got in touch with our own airbase some 200 miles away. We learned they were about to classify us as missing in action. Our squadron sent a B-26 after us and back at our own base the celebration started all over again.

The next day, November 11, was of course Armistice Day. Our squadron commander, a West Pointer with a keen sense of history, had arranged a celebration with the inhabitants of the village of Tille. The bonds forged between France and the U.S. down through the centuries were recalled, and the memory of the Marquis de Lafayette was revived yet again. Reporters from the G.I. newspaper *Stars & Stripes* came to interview and photograph our crew, sending the story to the hometown newspaper of each airman. We then returned to immediate anonymity and

Photo from news coverage of the crew's emergency landing on a road near Dijon. From the left, Jim, Herschel Tyson, Tom Mattax, Ralph Goldstein, Stan Adelman, and Jennings Van Flossen, with their B-26 in the background. Photo by Stars and Stripes.

50 Flak Bait

recalled the word of the poet who observed that "fame is fleeting."

I later teased Tom Maddax that while he received the Distinguished Flying Cross for his feat, the rest of us lost ten years of growth in the process.

The Battle of the Bulge

Every December my thoughts turn to the winter of 1944 and the desperate struggle between Allied and German forces that is remembered as the Battle of the Bulge. Beginning on December 16th, the German military attacked American and British forces on the Western front in Belgium, driving them back from their position in what appeared as a bulge in the front lines. It was the coldest winter in memory with unprecedented snowfall. The battle raged back and forth from mid-December in 1944 through

The B-26 Marauder ready for takeoff.

January 25, 1945, and more than one million men fought in the conflict.

The initial success of the D-Day landing had been extended as the Allies pushed inland, driving the Germans east. Our squadron advanced with the ground forces, and by the end of 1944 I had flown some 20 combat missions over Nazi Germany from our base in Beauvais.

Our routine in those days went something like this: In the afternoon, the flight crews would go to the operations office to study the alert list, which was the complete roster of crews ordered to fly the next day's mission. Upon seeing our names on the list, we would proceed to go to bed early in the hope that a good night's rest would result in our crew being fresh and alert for combat.

Four o'clock in the morning came all too soon, when an operations officer went from tent to tent waking the crews and urging us to dress warmly for the mission. First came the long flannel underwear, then coveralls, then a warm sheepskin-lined leather flight jacket, later to be followed by a flak suit, parachute, and other gear, all of which doubled the weight of the crewman.

Once dressed, we trudged through the snow and ice in below zero temperatures to reach the mess hall for breakfast. After the meal, we reported to the operations office for a briefing, where we received our routes, schedules, weather reports, a prediction of the temperature at altitude, reports on expected enemy opposition, and what to do if shot down. The latter advice included, if we were fortunate enough to be downed over France, to make every effort to fall under the care of the courageous French resistance movement, the members of which would attempt to protect us from capture.

After the briefing, we were taken by trucks to the airplanes to which we were assigned for the mission. Then we tried to relax before we were instructed to start our engines. This was no easy task while confronting the fact that in a short while we might we be wounded, dead, or made a prisoner of war. We waited near the aircraft. Often that winter, we would receive a command from operations—"Plus sixty"—which meant an hour's delay. It was not uncommon for the mission to be postponed two or even three times, followed by orders to "scrub" the mission. The resulting tension and uncertainty were hard on the crew.

In the Battle of the Bulge, Hitler had reinforced his fighter aircraft units and the strength of his ground forces for one last attempt to drive the Allies from the continent. He correctly predicted that the Allies would consider the dense forests of the Ardennes in Belgium as an unlikely point for a German attack. As a result, the thinly manned American troops there were taken by surprise.

To respond to the German advance, my B-26 bomber crew remained on the alert list for what seemed like ages. During the Battle of the Bulge, we were under orders to be prepared to carry out two perilous and mutually exclusive missions. The first was to carry out aggressive bombing warfare against the enemy, while the second was to be prepared to make a strategic withdrawal back to England in the face of the enemy. The situation could hardly have been more precarious. It called for the very best from both the aircraft and the crew members.

Tribute must be paid to the loyal ground crew members, who endured what can only be described as absolute hell in the sub-zero temperatures. Yet not a man failed to labor around the clock for days on end. Imagine having to lift into place 1,000-pound high-explosive bombs in cold so severe you could barely feel your fingers. One is reminded of the warrior of old who observed, "They also serve who only stand and wait."

Finally, after about two weeks of frigid futility, we received a favorable weather report for the next day. At last, we might be able to rise from our "hell on earth" and pursue the enemy.

The next morning, the day before Christmas Eve, I was awakened by the operations sergeant. I walked outside our tent and was greeted by a crisp, cold day, with the bluest sky I'd ever seen. Instead of the "plus 60" order, operations fired a Very pistol, which sent a flare into the air to signal that the mission was to proceed. We would take to the air.

This day we carried out what was known as a "maximum effort" mission, meaning that every aircraft capable of struggling off the frozen runway and every crew member not in the hospital was ordered to fly. Soon came the order to start engines. High drama if ever drama existed. I chose to take off in the navigator's seat rather than the nose gunner position, which was too vulnerable.

Our group fielded 54 medium bombers, escorted by P-38 Lightnings, P-47 Thunderbolts, P-51 fighters, as well as the fighter escorts of the Royal Air Force consisting of Hurricanes and Spitfires. As I saw these Allied fighter aircraft, I reflected that they might very well have flown in the Battle of Britain some four years earlier. Winston Churchill observed of the Battle of Britain, "Never in the field of human conflict have so many owed so much to so few."

Some two hours after takeoff we approached the target of the day, following the 391st Bomb Group directly ahead of us. By now I was in the Plexiglass nose of the craft, meaning I had a perfect view of what was happening ahead and to the side of our craft. The Germans had saved their fighters for this moment. Sixteen of the 54 bombers in the group ahead of us were in varying stages of being torn apart, with their crews adrift in the sky descending by parachute. As we watched in horror, we wondered if we awaited the same fate. Fortunately for us, our own fighter escort was taking a heavy toll on the attacking German fighters.

My log showed a bomb run of four minutes. It seemed like forever. But at last we were en route back to our base. Several of our planes were damaged by German flak and fighters, but none were lost. And while some of the crew members suffered severe injuries, we all made it back to Beauvais.

Later, strike photos and intelligence revealed that we had struck the target with precision, removing from combat a large number of enemy ground forces.

The mission was carried out on December 23, 1944. Military

historians have praised our efforts, concluding that it could even have been pivotal in the outcome of the war. Every man I knew who flew that day had the feeling he had earned his pay. But much more was yet to come before the war ended on May 8, 1945.

Homecoming

Curtis "Pop" Johnson was of that rare breed of men who could appear calm and cool under the most trying conditions. I first met Pop when we were assigned to live in the same pyramidal tent in an apple orchard near the English Channel in France. Although we were both from Texas, we were not very much alike, but we were destined to become warm friends and comrades in arms. Pop became known as Pop because he was the oldest combat crew member in the squadron. He was 24 and a veteran of some 50 aerial missions over enemy-held terrain. I was 20 and green as grass, having never felt the steel of our common enemy. He was a staff sergeant. I was a buck sergeant. On the ground, he was a mechanic, while in the air, he monitored the engines and the instruments and transferred fuel between tanks.

Although we served on different crews, Pop became my mentor and senior non-commissioned officer. He taught me how to hold my fire until enemy fighters were within our range and how to talk on the intercom without betraying the mortal fear that accompanied every man who flew in combat. He taught me to become alert to any unusual occurrence during the mission and to report those observations to intelligence officers at debriefing. Pop, who was from Mason, Texas, took obvious pride in witnessing the maturation of his young protégé. I tried to emulate him and to never fail him.

I once asked Pop what it was like to fly through a field of flak and if it was loud. Flak is a ball of steel pre-set to explode at the altitude of the attacking aircraft, so I should have known the answer.

"Oh Lord, Simpson," Pop replied, "Does it ever make a noise! It comes up there and explodes at your altitude, and the concussion lifts the airplane 10 feet. And it makes your old asshole draw up like a tobacco sack." Pop's colorful allusion referred to the small cloth sacks of loose tobacco, such as the brands Bull Durham or Duke's Mixture, which were closed by means of a drawstring.

During the Battle of the Bulge, Pop's record of missions grew, and it began to look as though he might beat the odds, fly a complete tour of 65 missions, accept a well-earned Distinguished Flying Cross, and go home to America with his war bride, a great English lady Pop had met before we moved the squadron from Essex, England, to Beauvais, France.

We made many of the same missions but never served on the same crew. Then came the day when Pop had flown 64 of his required missions. It came at a time when I was eligible for a short pass to Paris. We shook hands that night before lights out, and I remarked that by the time of my return, he might well have his 65th mission under his belt and would be ready to take his bride home to a land she had never seen.

"No, it will be my rotten luck to get killed on my 65th mission," he said.

Earlier, I had been assigned to the crew of the 65th mission of a Lieutenant Schultz, a pilot who could look forward to leaving combat upon his safe return. Because we were short of navigators and I had received aviation cadet training back in California, my commanding officer Colonel Newcomer had asked me to train as a bombardier-navigator. When I completed my training, the colonel promoted me to tech sergeant. However, most navigators were commissioned officers. When Lieutenant Schultz discovered that he would have a lowly sergeant as his navigator on his final mission, he grew quite upset.

"Why the hell are they assigning an enlisted man on my last mission?" he thundered. "This is my 65th mission, and I don't want anything to go wrong!" He might have even used stronger language than that. As in many endeavors in which the stakes are high, pilots could be superstitious and did not like surprises.

I replied, "Lieutenant, I didn't ask for this mission, and I'd be happy to go back to bed."

"Aw, it's too damn late. Let's just go," said Schultz.

At the end of the mission, when it was clear that Lieutenant Schultz would be able to leave Europe in one piece, he relaxed and apologized. "I'm sorry I gave you such a hard time," he said. "I was just worried about my last mission, and I was as nervous as a whore in church."

Pop Johnson was less fortunate. His last flight was a training mission at night. Our squadron had had disastrous results with a night combat mission in the summer of 1944, the first and only night combat mission carried out by my squadron. During the mission, three planes collided and the crews went down, including the squadron commander, Major George Simler, who survived after parachuting to the ground.

The squadron embarked on a night training exercise in the spring of 1945—Pop's 65th mission. Pop's comment as I was leaving for Paris turned out to be tragically prophetic. Pop Johnson died during this training mission in the dark sky over France.

Sergeant Curtis Johnson was laid to rest in a French field far from his native Texas. I will never forget him.

From the German Front to the French Riviera

After a crew member had flown 35 missions, the military assumed you were flak happy and needed a break from the stress of air combat.

When I had reached this threshold, I was summoned to the operations officer in my squadron, who told me that I had

A smile inspired by a weekend pass to Paris in 1944.

earned flak leave, but that instead of rest and relaxation, I was being sent to the German front.

The Air Force had instituted a policy of temporary duty for an air crew in the Air Corps to trade places with an infantry squad to promote better relations between air and ground forces. There had been some bad blood between the Air Corps and the infantry, and the exchange program was intended to alleviate this tension.

Occasionally, our aircraft would inadvertently drop bombs on our infantry on the ground. You could tell the nature of an infantry unit's experience with air support by the reception we got from ground troops. If our fighters in the 9th Air Force had destroyed an enemy tank that had threatened the ground troops, then you were warmly welcomed.

If, on the other hand, the infantry unit had been bombed by our planes—as occurred at St. Lo in France, killing the commanding officer, General Leslie McNair—you were as welcome as a cow patty in a punch bowl.

I was told to report to the 415th Infantry Regiment, 104th Infantry Division, which was commanded by a Texan, General Terry Allen, in Eschweiler, Germany. This was close to Aachen, just inside the German border. I thought I'd been pushed out of the frying pan and into the fire. Meanwhile, an infantry squadron was required to join our squadron in France.

Lieutenant Chauncey Weeks was co-pilot of my crew, so he drove our Jeep toward the German border. At one point, Weeks got sloppy with his driving and was stopped by the military police. The MP asked Weeks his rank and then wrote the lieutenant a ticket. We asked the nature of the offense.

"Officers are not permitted to drive," he informed us. Then he asked my rank, and when I replied that I was a staff sergeant, he said, "You're driving now."

So I drove the Jeep the rest of the way to Germany. I found it strange that the Army found it permissible for Lieutenant Weeks to fly a costly bomber, accept responsibility for a crew of six men, and fly them in harm's way to be shot at by the Germans, but that it was beneath the dignity of an officer to drive a Jeep.

I spent 10 days at the front in Germany. The noise was unnerving and it was terribly cold, even though we slept in the cellar of a bombed-out German house. We talked to ground troops about the importance of keeping air support well advised about the movements of the enemy and our own troops in order to avoid mishaps.

We were treated well at the front. I carried a .45 caliber pistol while I was there. The infantry offered me an opportunity to go behind enemy lines on night patrol to try to capture German soldiers for interrogation, but I passed. I figured I had adequate opportunity to get killed in the air.

I'll never forget hearing the big guns near the line opening up on the German division facing us across the Roer River. I attended a division meeting the day before the unit planned to cross the Roer River. This invasion of the German territory was one of the most extensive after D Day itself. I had no substantive duties because I had not been trained as an infantryman. Not to worry, I was issued a Thompson submachine gun as a personal weapon. We were told we were not required to cross the river in the pontoon boats in the first wave. This was optional. For the first time I encountered troops younger than I was. At the division briefing, General Cary Allen leveled with the troops, telling them that losses as a result of enemy fire were expected to be heavy. It was not to be a walk in the park.

With some trepidation and wonder as to whether I had lost my marbles, I accompanied a squad of infantrymen across the river. The Germans had dug in with trenches in an area of Duran previously a housing subdivision. There in a trench just a few yards behind their front line lay a German soldier, obviously dead. He looked to be 17, younger than my 20 years. He was pale of color and his blue eyes stared out. It occurred to me there was scant little difference between him and me except he had taken one of our infantryman's bullets right between the eyes. I thought then that there must be a better way of resolving international disputes.

I returned to my squadron in France, and we later moved to

Le Culot in Belgium. After about a dozen additional missions, my crew and I were finally granted flak leave in the resort city of Nice on the French Riviera. Gunders Wonders, as the crew was called, received 10 days on the Mediterranean. We were told to report to the flight line at 0800 to catch a C-47 for Nice.

Out of habit, I looked for my parachute on board the aircraft. I couldn't find it. When I called out to a tech sergeant, asking the whereabouts of my parachute, he informed me that only the crew received parachutes.

"That's a hell of note," I said. "If we encounter engine trouble, the crew bails out and we go down with the plane." The tech sergeant laughed and conceded that I had a point. Still, no parachute was forthcoming.

Once in Nice, we were lodged at the Angleterre Hotel. We were forbidden to "eat on the economy" in Nice, which is to say, we could not eat in restaurants. The French people were suffering from a shortage of food as it was, and the military didn't want a bunch of hungry G.I.s buying up what little food was available.

In hindsight, the whole policy of flak leave may have been a mistake. Once submerged in battle, the danger you were exposed to became routine. But once we were away from the daily stress of war, I no longer took it for granted. Returning to the rigors of combat in Belgium was unnerving. During the five minutes before takeoff on my first mission, I sweated blood. It took a while to readjust.

I was once on a mission riding in the nose of the airplane to navigate by sighting landmarks. Suddenly, from another squadron above and ahead of me two parachutes blossomed. I thought that maybe I'd botched the navigating and our bomber was in the wrong place. I later learned that the two crewmen bailed out as a result of fear. They just couldn't cope with the stress of the mission in progress. I was told they were both court-martialed for cowardice in the face of combat.

For 10 days we escaped all that. While I was on the Riviera, I went out on the water in a motor boat. We went swimming.

Jim on flak leave at the French Riviera, April 1945.

62　Flak Bait

There were attractive French women sunbathing on the beach. They were quite friendly toward the American soldiers, but the language barrier was difficult to overcome. That reminds me of the Bill Maulden cartoon of two American G.I.s walking down the street in a French village. Everyone on the street looked just like one of the American soldiers. The caption read: "I believe this is the little town where my Daddy was stationed in the First World War."

On the promenade in Nice in April 1945. From the left, Joe Gallant of Maine, Jim Simpson, and Frank Convertine of Pittsburgh enjoy flak leave.

France Revisited

During my service in the European Theater of World War II, I took care to learn the history of the various villages where I was stationed. Soissons, Beauvais, and other towns became quite familiar to many of us. I recalled from my high school studies that Soissons was the site of a significant battle during World War I.

A few weeks before we were to occupy the air base at Beauvais-Tille, a pitched battle had occurred. Beauvais was the larger town, and on its outskirts was the village of Tille, closest to the air base. As mentioned previously, because the German Luftwaffe operated from Beauvais-Tille, my own squadron had bombed the air base and the town of Beauvais in advance of the invasion by the Allied forces. Nonetheless, the villagers were quite friendly, recognizing that we had come as liberators and not as occupiers. We became acquainted with many of the villagers.

Although they had suffered great privation at the hands of the German army, the townspeople were very accommodating to us. We arrived in September of 1944 during the apple harvest, and we pitched our tents in the wooded area surrounding Beauvais. The farmers took no offense when we gathered some of their ripening apples. One could read in their faces that they were pleased to receive the Americans and other Allies. We stayed in Beauvais through almost the entire winter of 1944-45, which was very severe.

The woods around Beauvais provided us with the firewood we needed to stay warm. At times the highlight of our day was enjoying a cup of thin bouillon soup heated on a potbelly stove in the center of our tent. Meanwhile, we shared our meager rations with the French people, who were most appreciative.

In December of that year, a lieutenant in the squadron named Joe Moore began systematically collecting candy bars, gum, cookies, and other sweets from the men. He had taken an interest in the children of Beauvais, many of whom had been

64   Flak Bait

orphaned by the war. On Christmas Eve, he organized a party for all the citizens of the town, and with the help of others in the squadron, prepared a small gift for each child. The party was held in the squadron mess hall, where there was a lighted Christmas tree and a turkey dinner with all the trimmings had been prepared. All this occurred in spite of the fact that the squadron was flying two missions a day to thwart the advance of the Germans in the Ardennes. Joe Moore, a co-pilot, also sang Christmas carols. Other crew members helped with the entertainment, and those men who were fathers were especially touched by the event. At least for a few hours, the agony of war was diminished for the townspeople. Sadly, a few days later Lieutenant Moore was killed during a bombing mission over enemy terrain. Every December I remember our makeshift Christmas party in the village of Beauvais during the winter of 1944.

When Connie and I were in France in the late 1970s, we returned to Beauvais and Tille to renew old memories. Departing Paris from the Gare du Nord railway terminal, we met a young man on the train who inquired if we were on a pilgrimage. I explained that I had flown missions from the air base in Tille, and he expressed an appreciation for our efforts in the liberation of his country. When we arrived in Beauvais, the young man assisted us in finding a taxi to take us to Tille.

Tille was the site of a prominent Catholic church familiar to us. I could recall using the steeple of the church as a landmark to help navigate the B-26 bombers returning from missions over Germany. Arriving at the now modern Tille airport, we could find little that was familiar. When a villager overheard our discussion, he volunteered to find someone who remembered the days of the American occupation. Soon we had a companion and guide who took us in hand. In spite of the language barrier, I brought out a book containing the history of the squadron and pointed out a photograph of the squadron mess hall. Our guide then found the battered structure that had previously served as our mess hall and, prior to that, a hangar for the Luftwaffe aircraft.

The people of Tille had not fared well under the German occupation. Our guide, whose name was Georges Crucifix, had once been mayor of Tille. A congenial host, he took us to his home and introduced us to his charming wife and twin daughters. By great coincidence, he had served in the French air force and been held by the Germans as a prisoner of war. Georges had a considerable collection of model aircraft covering the wall of his living room. He opened a bottle of champagne, and we made our time together a festive occasion. It was a wonderful visit, and we vowed to meet again.

Years later in 1994, on the occasion of the 50th anniversary of our squadron's deployment at Beauvais, we joined a squadron reunion in France. Upon reaching Tille, I inquired about Georges Crucifix and was told that he had died. However, my source explained that Georges' son was on hand for the event. The son, also named Georges, recalled that his father had told him of our earlier visit. Georges the younger brought us up to date on the news of the village and served as our guide, as his father had done decades before. A small air museum had been established in Tille, and a monument was erected as a memorial to the American soldiers stationed there whose lives were lost in the war.

When we reached Beauvais, there was a reception held in our honor at city hall. Champagne was served, and many toasts were made celebrating the return of the Americans.

My Friend Manuel

In January of 1945, some five months before victory in Europe, Manuel Escamilla of Laredo, Texas, joined my squadron as a radio operator and gunner. He was fresh from combat crew training at Barksdale Field in Shreveport, Louisiana.

While Manuel was courageous, he was terrified of being

shot at in an airplane. I could sense on a training mission that he was nervous to the point of having an adverse affect on his performance in combat. Now, it is disturbing to be trapped in a long cylinder of aluminum while German gunners fire away at you, intent on your destruction. So it was perfectly understandable that our crew members could succumb to shell shock or combat fatigue. I realized the need to get Manuel settled down. I pointed out to him that I had survived dozens of missions without harm and that he could do the same. While Manuel was a couple of years older than I was, he had carried the burden of racism. Because I spoke high school-level Spanish and I was also from Texas, we had much in common and became friends. He agreed to help me with my Spanish, and I helped him get accustomed to life in the squadron. He became a reliable crew member and occasionally served on my crew.

One of the planes in our squadron was named *Flak Bait*. The plane was already celebrated for its many close brushes with disaster by the time I joined the squadron. Even then we recognized that *Flak Bait*, if she survived the war, was destined to earn a place in history. For that reason, almost all the flight crews in the squadron were given an opportunity to fly a mission on the aircraft. I flew several missions aboard her. *Flak Bait* completed 202 missions, more than any Allied aircraft in the Second World War.

By the end of the war, it had sustained more than 2,000 flak hits or bullet holes. *Flak Bait* returned from bombing missions twice with one engine disabled and once with an engine on fire. It lost its electrical system once and its hydraulic system twice, and participated in bombing missions in support of D-Day and the Battle of the Bulge. The forward section of the fuselage is on display at the Smithsonian Institution's National Air and Space Museum.

On March 18, 1945, Manuel and I flew a mission to a target near Wiesbaden, Germany. Manuel was assigned to his regular crew and I was serving with Gunder's Wonders, a crew that owed its name to its pilot, Herb Gunderson. Prior to this mission, the squadron commander had admonished all the pilots to fly in a tight formation to take full advantage of the defenses provided by the fighter planes that would accompany our bombers. The runway at our base in Beauvais was like a sheet of ice that day.

I was flying in the nose of our B-26 as our planes clustered together in a tight formation for the mission to Germany. Suddenly, one bomber started moving perilously close to the lead bomber. I sensed extreme danger, and within seconds, the lead ship was struck by its left wingman. A violent explosion followed the collision, and fire engulfed still a third aircraft. All three bombers were lost in a single instant. Only one crew member, the lead pilot Alex Olaf Cordes, survived, saved by the

The most famous B-26, Flak Bait, on display at the Smithsonian Air and Space Museum in Washington, D.C. It acquired more than 2,000 flak and bullet holes during 202 combat missions.

armor plate behind the pilot's seat and the partial opening of his parachute. The 18 other crewmen were killed that Sunday morning, including Sergeant Manuel Escamilla.

The cause of the crash was determined to be the inexperience of one of the new pilots. What a tragic loss of 18 young men. We will never know what outstanding contributions they might have made later had they survived.

After the war, I should have traveled to Laredo to speak to Manuel's family, but got wrapped up in getting an education and starting a career. Some 25 years after the end of the war I was in Laredo with my family. I consulted the phone directory and found a listing for Manuel Escamilla. I knew, of course, that it was Manuel's father. I phoned the number and asked the man who answered if he had had a son in the Air Force in the war.

"Yes," he replied. "But the boy was killed."

"I know," I said, "because I had the privilege of serving with him."

"I must see you," said Mr. Escamilla.

Soon the elder Manuel and his son, Roberto, arrived at my hotel. They also brought a reporter from *The Laredo Times*. I talked to them about the times I spent with Manuel in France and his service in the squadron. Mr. Escamilla was thrilled to hear from a first-hand source that his son had served bravely and was a true patriot. He repeated several times, "I just wish Momma was still alive. She would have loved to talk to you about our son."

At that point I deeply regretted waiting 25 years to contact the family.

Many times since the war I have reflected on the fact that Manuel died defending the concept that all men are created equal. Manuel had fought for this principle, although as a Mexican American, he was not always the beneficiary of it.

In December of 1972 my daughter, Simone, was struck by a car while crossing a street in Laredo. She had gone on a trip there sponsored by the University of Texas, where she was a student. The only person I knew to call was Roberto Escamilla, Manuel's brother. Within the hour, he was at my daughter's bedside at the hospital. Roberto soon called me to assure me that Simone's injuries were not life threatening. I deeply appreciated his concern.

I thought of the Escamilla family again in 1994, when I visited a monument to the men of the 451st Bomb Squadron who had lost their lives in the liberation of France. There on a bronze plaque at the Beauvais-Tille airbase was the name of my old friend, "Manuel Escamilla."

College Years

A final photo in uniform: Jim and Bob Simpson, Temple, Texas, 1945.

Entering UT

I was fortunate to be among the first combat veterans of World War II to be released from active duty at the close of the war in Europe. When the Germans surrendered, I had accumulated 59 of the required 65 combat missions over enemy terrain. My time in the service was shortly more than three years, enough to turn my attention to other matters. On the way back from Europe, I became familiar with the great privileges granted by the G.I. Bill of Rights. This was a real turning point in my life. I was still in excellent health and had saved some of my earnings, and now I had earned the educational benefits afforded by the G.I. bill.

I returned to Texas and Fort Sam Houston in early July 1945. Once I arrived at the base, I was advised that if I was so inclined, I could receive an honorable discharge. Otherwise, my service would be extended by another six months. I chose to get on with my life.

I went home to Copperas Cove, some 140 miles north of San Antonio, and my parents welcomed me back into the old room I had occupied until Pearl Harbor took me away. Mother, dad, and I were discussing my future one day when my father said he had heard there were openings for truck drivers over at Belton. My mother was outraged, declaring, "That baby is not going to be a truck driver. He's going to become a lawyer! He will attend the University of Texas." When my mother spoke her mind, her words became law.

Once again, I resorted to hitchhiking as a means of travel. I picked up my high school transcript, made copies of my military records, and presented myself at the registrar's office at the University of Texas in Austin in July of 1945. Gaining admission was not a difficult task if one had a high school diploma and was otherwise qualified to attend. Once I was admitted, the registrar's office gave me a list of rooming houses where I might find suitable lodging.

I walked from the campus to 2100 Rio Grande, an old two-story rooming house. As I mounted the steps at 2100 a voice called out to me, "Hey, Fly Boy, come on over here." It was another turning point in my life. The voice was that of Charles W. Britt, who had been a student at UT for about one year following the Battle of Attu in the Aleutian Islands. Charlie had been wounded, though not critically, and was anxious to make the acquaintance of another veteran of the war.

Britt had fallen upon hard times financially and he presumed correctly that a recently discharged vet would have a few dollars to rub together from his mustering out pay. Two habits of Britt generated a demand for spending money — smoking and consuming beer, pastimes principally engaged in at Scholz Garten, a landmark 1866 beer garden south of the campus popular with students, faculty, and politicians. He suggested that for the mere cost of a cold bottle of beer I could avail myself of his learned counsel about how best to make my way around the shoals of the University. It was a hot summer day, and we soon found refuge at one of the tables of the ancient beer garden.

After Britt was served a bottle of cold beer, he made further inquiry. "Could you spring for a pack of cigarettes?" I was not a smoker, but I could afford a pack of cigarettes, which cost 15 cents. It developed that Britt had joined the Army Infantry even before the outbreak of hostilities. The Battle of Attu left him with a minor hearing deficit. I learned that he had been a buck sergeant in an infantry company, and that as a high school graduate he was something of an oddity in the pre-World War II Army. Like me, he was seeking a better way of making one's way through the world than either of us could have aspired to before the war.

"What do you want to do?" my newfound friend asked.

I said I thought I would study aeronautical engineering.

Charlie immediately denounced the idea, asking if I had ever troubled myself to look at the catalog for the College of Engineering. I soon concluded that if I was to survive the brave new world confronting Britt and me and millions of other veterans, that I would have to rely on my verbal skills rather than my knowledge of engineering, mathematics, and science. In a heartbeat I changed from engineering to pre-law at the urging of my new friend.

I still had not found a place of habitation. Britt suggested I take a vacant room until his then-current roommate moved out, whereupon I could move in with him. I had been accustomed to the comradeship of other non-commissioned officers, and this had become an important part of my life.

The G.I. Bill provided a subsistence allowance of $70 a month. Month after month this amount proved inadequate to Britt because of his addiction to cigarettes, a habit I had not acquired. Toward the end of each month I noticed that Britt roamed about the old rooming house seeking discarded cigarettes. When that source ran out, he issued a plaintive cry, "Your old buddy is totally out of cigarettes." Soon he was bumming cigarettes not just by the pack, but by the carton. I made it plain to him I was no longer going to be responsible for his nicotine habit. This proved to be very effective. He soon cut in half his demand for nicotine.

When the Christmas holidays rolled around I went home to Copperas Cove and Britt went back to his home in Alvin. It was interesting to note that after a few days absence from one another we were happy to be back together again.

I never acquired the nicotine habit, and I indeed reduced my demand for cold beer. Admission to law school required three years of undergraduate work. Britt entered the law school before I did, but by going to summer school, I soon caught up with him in academics.

The Water Was Cold But the Rock Was Hot

We each found the law school to be much more demanding than our undergraduate studies. In law school we were joined by one other conspirator, William Goldap, who was also a former sergeant. Goldap had a great sense of humor and an inquiring mind. For instance he would say to me, "Simpson, you would be handsome if it weren't for your face." On other occasions he would remark, "Simpson, you can't help how you look but you could at least stay home." Fortunately, our good nature prevented any of us from taking undue offense.

We all took a great interest in issues and events of the times. Each of us was offended by the commonly accepted practice of racial discrimination. This placed our lot with the liberal element of political thought.

I recall one year in which Goldap found his way to the State Democratic Convention held in San Antonio. There he fell among evil companions who plied him with hard drink over his objections, of course. His vociferous conduct attracted the attention of some of the Alamo City's finest. This resulted in his apprehension with all the attendant consequences, much of which was recorded for history in the local newspaper, *The San Antonio Light*. Rather than being embarrassed, Bill wore this incident as a badge of honor. But it did nothing to embellish his fame as a civil rights advocate.

Joe Metze, a business major and another resident of 2100 Rio Grande, had become accustomed to drinking beer on his own at the Esquire Club. On one occasion, as was his wont, he fell to drinking with other patrons, staying until closing time. Joe came waltzing out of the Esquire Club feeling no pain, but with his vision slightly impaired. As he emerged onto 6th Street, his eye fell upon a black and white four-door sedan. Perceiving it to be a taxi, he got in the back seat and demanded to be taken to 2100 Rio Grande and be quick about it. The uniformed driver quickly transported Joe to the Travis County Jail instead. Some taxi. It fell to my lot to answer the phone when Joe called announcing his present predicament. Fortunately, I was able to make adequate excuse for the conduct of my good friend, and he was thereupon released without much ado.

During my UT days, Barton Springs was my favorite hangout. There I encountered another triumvirate composed of

J. Frank Dobie, folklorist, Walter Prescott Webb, the noted author on the subject of the West, and Roy Bedichek, the Texas naturalist and environmentalist.

Their favorite place of repose was a huge rock which emerged from the cold springs of Barton's bearing the name of Bedichek's Rock, which inspired the poem: "Bedichek sat on Bedichek's Rock. The water was cold but the rock was hot." Needless to say, the company of these three distinguished men had a much more salutary effect on our young triumvirate than the Esquire Club.

Despite predictions to the contrary, my two friends and I managed to finish the UT Law School and, in an even greater surprise, we all passed the state bar exam. We were admitted to the practice of law on September 16, 1950.

To our consternation, the three of us found that the legal profession was not unduly thrilled at the prospect of our joining the ranks of practicing lawyers. We soon found that a burning desire to cure the ills of society was not sufficient to land oneself a coveted position in a prestigious law firm. A good heart and a sincere desire to make the world a better place were poor substitutes for having earned a Phi Beta Kappa key or experience on the *Texas Law Review*.

The fortunate ones were young lawyers whose fathers before them had founded successful law practices, but I certainly did not fit this mold. My precious father was able to loan me enough money to buy a dark blue suit with a little money left over to travel the entire state in pursuit of employment. Most law firms where I applied carefully told me that what they needed was more clients, not more lawyers.

While tramping the streets of the major cities of Texas, my eye fell upon an article in the newspaper pointing out that applications were being taken from recent law school graduates for positions as a special agent of the FBI. I felt surely that some of my peccadilloes of the past would emerge from the careful investigation the Bureau performed on all applicants. Nevertheless, I filed my application, putting as good a face as possible on my background, with some emphasis on the fact I had served for three years in the U.S. Air Force and that I saw combat on 59 bombing missions over Nazi Germany. Surely this would attest to my loyalty as a citizen. Without much hope of success with the FBI, I continued to seek a place to hang my hat.

The FBI Years

Telegram from J. Edgar Hoover

My first real contact with Galveston County came in early January 1951. I had grown up in Coryell County, some 240 miles northwest of Galveston. The economy for newly minted lawyers was not ideal. Most law firms with whom I had contact after being licensed in September 1950, were not hiring new lawyers, at least not with my meager credentials.

After striking out in virtually every major city in Texas, I determined to open my own office. My mother and father, who lived in Temple at the time, were kind enough to help me launch a practice, but their resources as we emerged from the Great Depression and World War II were severely limited.

I borrowed enough to pay the expenses of opening an office plus about one month's overhead. My ambition far exceeded my hope for success. Nonetheless, I shared an office with an older lawyer in a hole-in-the-wall type arrangement in La Marque, Texas. I had no secretary and could carry my law library in two hands.

The profession and the community took little note of my debut. My contemporaries at the bar were unable to be of help as they themselves were struggling to get a foothold in law practice. I had totally forgotten that a few months earlier I had applied to the FBI for a job as special agent. I recall thinking at the time that surely the Bureau's customarily thorough investigation would reveal some past skullduggery on my part that would eliminate me from consideration. But lo and behold, as I sat in my modest office with scant little to do, I received a telegram from J. Edgar Hoover, Director of the FBI. Hoover offered me a position as special agent at a salary of $5,000 per year. This offer exceeded my hopes.

I immediately telegraphed my acceptance, lest J. Edgar Hoover might reconsider the offer. I had so little law practice that it was not a big job to close the office. I sold or gave away the paltry office furniture and books I had naively acquired. Then I went to see my mother and father in Temple. My daddy drove me over to Waco to a men's store where I acquired a suit and overcoat. I then took a train to Washington, D.C. I didn't have the money for a first class berth with sleeping accommodations, so I sat upright every mile of the way to the nation's capital.

I had so little money to subsist on that I would jump off the train at major terminals to find an inexpensive diner where I could make my meager resources go farther.

I was sworn in as a special agent on November 11, 1950. The Bureau had neglected to tell me that I would not receive my first two week's pay—that was to be set aside so I could return home in the event the Bureau decided to terminate me for some reason. That made for an ominous start to my career as a special agent.

Despite my impoverished state, it was a heady experience to be living in the nation's capital and attending the FBI Academy, in nearby Quantico, Virginia. Quantico was not only the home of the Bureau Academy, but also major facilities of the U.S. Marine Corps.

The training involved the maintenance and use of firearms, preservation of evidence, understanding each of the statutes granting jurisdiction to the FBI, fingerprinting, use of the FBI laboratory, and countless other subjects essential to effective law enforcement.

Following graduation, all of the newly minted special agents were gathered in a large classroom where an Assistant Director of the Bureau read out our new assignments. My assignment was to the field office in Chicago under the command of a legendary figure, George McSwain.

Before leaving Washington, one last item was on the agenda—a brief meeting with the director, J. Edgar Hoover. I must observe that he did not seek my counsel on the affairs of the Bureau. He was cordial and wished me well on my first assignment.

The train trip from Grand Central Station in Washington to

Chicago took about 24 hours. I had the address of the field office and almost no other useful information. I had no notion where I might find living quarters. I thought of seeking refuge in the YMCA, but I learned it was full and had a long waiting list.

Jim in front of the United States Supreme Court Building during his FBI training in Washington, D.C.

I ended up going to the old Harrington Hotel, where one could have a room for less than two dollars per night if one were willing to reside in cramped quarters with modest furnishings. It was far from the Waldorf Astoria.

I was teamed up with a veteran agent, Frank J. Reilly, who had served as an agent for 10 years and was thoroughly acquainted with the vast majority of situations one might encounter. Frank and I went to the Bureau garage, where we checked out a 1947 Pontiac sedan. We had been assigned to an investigation requiring that a number of leads be pursued in the city, after which we were to report back to the office.

Frank had me doing the driving, and we were on a major street when the radio connecting us with headquarters blared forth an urgent announcement to the effect that an armed robbery had just occurred at Irving Park National Bank. It occurred to me to try to determine just where we were when, lo and behold, I looked at a street sign informing me that we were on Irving Park Road.

I had visions of my being decorated and promoted on my first day of duty if only we could apprehend the bank robber. Alas, it was not to be. Within a few minutes the radio advised that the robbers had already been arrested by agents of the FBI and members of the Chicago Police Department.

My assignment in the Chicago office was to the criminal squad, and Chicago had its share of criminal activity. It seemed that practically every hoodlum on the lam had fancied he could seek refuge in Chicago. Oftentimes paid informants, in exchange for some coin of the realm, would provide us with the location of one or more fugitives from justice. At first, making arrests was a matter fraught with apprehension. With the passage of time, I gained more and more confidence.

Meanwhile, the training program continued unabated. One full day each month was set aside for training in firearms and techniques for apprehending dangerous criminals without endangering the public. This training was held on the Illinois-Wisconsin border at a National Guard facility known as Camp Ripley. One Saturday it fell my duty to take five other agents, together with arms and ammo to the training camp. Because we were to receive instruction in the use of pistols, shotguns, submachine guns, and other weapons, we were armed to the teeth. When I noticed we were in danger of running out of gas, I pulled into a service station by the side of the road. After filling up the car and paying for the gas, we departed. We were a scruffy lot that Saturday morning, and before long the siren and flashing red lights of a Chicago Police Department cruiser was pulling us over.

I told the officer we were all FBI agents and were bound for Camp Ripley. After checking my credentials, the officer let us go on our way with a fairly stern lecture informing us that we should not roam around looking like a band of ruffians. Fortunately, no official report was made of the incident, and I was spared any further embarrassment.

An interesting footnote to the story is that the person who reported us to the police was the same fellow from whom we had bought a tank of gas. The poor guy phoned the police to report that a car full of six unshaven thugs traveling with machine guns and all manner of weapons was heading north toward Wisconsin.

When things got boring on the criminal squad, we would occasionally be assigned tasks in the division of internal security. These often involved investigations of the Communist Party and the Socialist Workers Party. While I was on surveillance of the brother of a national leader of the Communist Party, the subject decided to leave Chicago and take his family on a vacation. This meant that I and three other agents were required to take a paid vacation. Our route of travel took us north into the lake region of Illinois. Our subject rented a cabin on Fox Lake and we, of course, did the same. Coincidentally, the subject enjoyed much the same outdoor activities as I enjoyed. We spent much time canoeing and fishing on the lake and going to a bowling alley. This surveillance was totally unproductive, and two weeks later I was back in the field office sporting a healthy suntan.

After nine months of duty in Chicago, I was ordered to the

field office in Minneapolis, Minnesota, an assignment that would change my life.

The Ten Most Wanted

In November 1951, after I had spent a year as a special agent in the Chicago office of the FBI, I was ordered to report to the Special Agent in Charge in Minneapolis, Minnesota. This office was headed up by the legendary W. G ("Guy") Banister. He was truly the stuff of legends.

Rumor had it that Banister had taken a bullet that had been intended for FBI Director J. Edgar Hoover. Banister had been employed by the New Orleans police department at the time, and the Crescent City was home to a number of high profile criminals. A raid was planned on the headquarters of the New Orleans underworld. J. Edgar Hoover headed the group of law enforcement officers, and in the course of events, Banister demonstrated tremendous courage.

On his return to Washington, D.C., Hoover contacted Banister, who did not have the credentials or the level of education customarily required for entry-level agents. He offered Banister an immediate commission as a special agent, which was unheard of in the Bureau. When the New Orleans policeman arrived in Washington, Hoover placed a memo into the file of agent Banister, which read, according to legend, "For so long as I am director of the FBI, this man shall hold no position lower than that of Special Agent in Charge."

As a result, Banister could do no wrong, and promotions came rapidly. The Minneapolis field office covered three states—Minnesota and North and South Dakota—and the office was considered quite a plum. In reporting to Mr. Banister on my arrival, I noted that he carried twin ivory paneled .38 caliber revolvers.

For some reason, the Twin Cities area had more than its

share of communists and communist sympathizers. It fell my lot to be assigned to the security squad which dealt with investigation into the Communist Party and its rival, the even more radical Socialist Workers Party. As I was single, the powers that be felt free to send me on road trips throughout the tri-state area. This was not without its advantages. While outside of his headquarters city, an agent received an additional nine dollars per day as a subsistence allowance. At the time, an agent's annual salary was only $5,000 per year. Hence, the extra nine dollars per diem was a godsend.

In many of the small towns in the tri-state area, I could rent a room for a dollar a night in a family residence, and for another three dollars I could have three square meals. This may have been the beginning of the concept of the bed and breakfast. The FBI maintained close contact with members of the general public who had at one time served the Bureau. I called on one such person in the quaint lakeside village of Deer Lake in the beautiful lake region of northern Minnesota. We became instant friends, and he insisted I stay in his home while working in the area. He was a source of much good information as well. One night at his home, I was awakened at 2:00 A.M. Guy Banister, the Agent in Charge, was on the phone instructing me to immediately proceed to Fargo, North Dakota, where it was believed that one of the Ten Most Wanted criminals was to be found. In 20 below zero temperature, I immediately pulled on my long-flannel underwear, my suit, and storm coat, and proceeded to Fargo on roads that were now a cake of ice. Once there, I was to contact the chief of detectives and assist in the apprehension of this infamous fugitive.

I checked with the chief of detectives, emphasizing the importance of being absolutely correct in our procedures. After all, this was one of America's Ten Most Wanted. The chief assured me that the subject he had seen was indeed the fugitive. Upon further cross-examination, the detective steadfastly maintained that we were on the verge of apprehending one of America's most dangerous criminals. At his office, we found a set of the fugitive's fingerprints and proceeded to the hotel that was serving as his hideaway. Hoover had a clear rule that required the FBI agent on such an apprehension be the dominant and most visible force.

Although the chief was older and more experienced than I, protocol required that I lead the effort. Going to the room of the fugitive, I pounded on the door and announced "FBI and Fargo P.D. Open this door immediately!" Out walked a bleary-eyed citizen, whom I placed under arrest, fitting him with a pair of handcuffs. Meanwhile, he demanded to know why he was under arrest, at which time I accused him of being the fugitive. He offered to produce all kinds of documents proving his identity. I asked him if he would permit himself to be fingerprinted, stating that I had a set of prints that would settle the matter. Having completed the task, I realized immediately that the man in custody was not one of the most wanted men in America.

I apologized profusely, and implored him to chalk it up to careless work on our part—and to my youthful inexperience. Fortunately for me, the man was more generous than just. He told me to forget about it, explaining that now he had something to tell the Rotary Club at their next Wednesday meeting in Farmington, New Mexico, where he was an agricultural implement salesman. I reported the entire episode to the Special Agent in Charge in Minneapolis, and thereafter, following a good breakfast, I went to back to bed, fearful of my future as an FBI agent.

The Deserter

There were many things about my service as a special agent in the FBI that I could never have predicted. Finding myself tracking a Sioux Indian fugitive up into the mountains of the South Dakota Indian country was one of them.

It has long been part of the jurisdiction of the FBI to have investigating authority over crimes committed on government reservations, including Indian reservations. I was an agent during the Korean War, and at the time it was quite common for young Indian men to go "over the hill" after being conscripted. In my opinion, this was not out of disloyalty or lack of patriotism. It was a cultural matter. All they had known for their entire lives was life on the reservation. Family was a very important institution, and when they were separated from family it was an alien and traumatizing experience. Not to mention the fact that young Native Americans were likely to be ambivalent about fighting a war on the other side of the planet when they were frequently deprived of such basic needs as education, health care, and regular employment here in America. They might reasonably ask why they should be hauled to another continent to shoot at people who had never addressed them with the racial slurs and pejoratives that Indians routinely encountered right here in the United States.

In any event, it was not uncommon for Indian soldiers to be absent without leave or to fail to return after an authorized absence. They were then classified as deserters, and their arrest followed as a matter of course. While a law enforcement officer would normally need an arrest warrant, that's not necessary to apprehend a deserter.

Customarily, Indians on the reservation had two names—their legal name and their Indian name, such as Crow Foot or Little Bear. In 1951 I was assigned the task of apprehending a deserter named Rain in the Face. I have forgotten his legal name, but I will never forget my encounter with Rain in the Face.

An informant told me of his whereabouts out in the woods on the Rosebud Sioux Indian Reservation in west South Dakota. I located his cabin and called out his name. Rain in the Face emerged from the cabin, and with little fanfare, I took him into custody. He was about 20 years old and had been drafted into the military. Undoubtedly, he was destined to be sent to Korea, an unhappy prospect for someone who had not ventured very far off the reservation.

I explained to him that my duty required me to take him to Aberdeen, South Dakota, where I was to turn him over to Army authorities. I further explained to him that it was a three-hour trip, and I regretted having to handcuff him or use other restraints for the long journey. At this point, I told him I would forego the handcuffs upon his promise that he would make no effort to escape.

Rain in the Face, who was of medium build and about my size, then made a solemn oath that he would not attempt to escape my custody. Throughout all this, the young man was courteous and not at all confrontational.

After driving a couple of hours, I noticed the gas gauge on the Bureau car indicated that we were almost empty. When we stopped for gas, Rain in the Face asked my permission to go to the restroom, which I granted. As I watched him approach the restroom, he suddenly broke and ran. I followed and attempted a flying tackle, which was to no avail. Rain in the Face escaped.

I now had a severe problem. J. Edgar Hoover, Director of the FBI, had a standing policy that he would fire any agent who negligently allowed the escape of a prisoner in custody. Rain in the Face was not the only person in trouble.

I promptly returned to the reservation, where I found the tribal chief, himself a federal employee, and explained to him that my job was in jeopardy unless I could immediately recapture Rain in the Face. The chief well understood the situation and agreed to help me.

He took out a map in his office showing the mountainous terrain in which I might locate the fugitive. I then drove the Bureau car as far as the rugged terrain would permit. Then I got out on foot and hiked up into the mountains until I found a small primitive hut in a densely wooded area, just as the chief had predicted.

Inside the hut I found Rain in the Face, and I placed him under arrest. "No more Mr. Nice Guy," I told him. Then I explained to him that if I were to report his escape, he would be prosecuted both for desertion and for escaping federal custody. I also advised him that I, too, would be in trouble if my superiors learned of his escape. So we struck a bargain. Rain in the

Face promised to keep his mouth shut about his escapade if I would do the same.

This time, I did place him in handcuffs, and I successfully delivered the prisoner to Army authorities. As a deserter, he probably received six months in the stockade, a reduction in rank, and the loss of some of his Army pay. I was never to see him again.

Throughout the episode, I was determined to keep from being fired. However, it was about this time that I decided to retire from federal service. So intimidating was J. Edgar Hoover's threat that I waited at least 10 years before I told another soul about the escape of Rain in the Face. Apparently, he remained equally discreet.

On the Trail of Communists in Minnesota

In Minneapolis, a woman named Grace Carlson had been executive director of the Socialist Workers Party. Prior to her life as a socialist, she had been a devout member of her local church when she became enamored of one of the leaders of the S.W.P. He enticed her into joining the party, and she later became manager of the Minnesota branch.

When an agent wanted to interview an officer of the Socialist Workers Party or the Communist Party, he had to first get authority from the Bureau back in Washington. I secured this authority and made my first contact with Miss Carlson. She was less than thrilled to meet an agent of the Bureau. At first, she was highly agitated. I sought to put her mind at ease by telling her I was not arresting her, but I merely wanted to learn whatever information she was willing to divulge about the work of the Party. She acknowledged her membership, but said she would not identify any other person in the party. But by the time our first interview ended, she was more relaxed and less defensive. I asked if I might feel free to call on her again, and she said yes, that would be all right.

A few weeks later, I did seek to re-interview her, and found her much more cordial. It developed that she had had some misgivings about the wisdom of her conversion to socialism and had thought of leaving the party even before my first contact. Ultimately, over a period of weeks, she agreed to change allegiance, and to become an informant for the Bureau. For an agent to "turn around" an officer of the Party was something of a coup. I reported the sequence of events to Mr. Banister, who uncharacteristically exhibited much pleasure. Ms. Carlson, gradually over a period of months, provided a great deal of background and intelligence to the Bureau.

There was a culture in the FBI that tended to discourage employees from forming friendships with persons outside the Bureau. Also, if an agent were to marry an employee of the Bureau one or the other would have to resign. There was in the office at Minneapolis an unusually attractive young lady who caught my eye. I inquired of a fellow agent as to whether this lady might be responsive to my attentions. He informed me, incorrectly as I found out, that Connie Griffith was already spoken for and that in fact she was quite often brought to work by an admirer. This was disappointing, as I had about summoned up enough courage to ask her for a date. With the passage of time I found that my friend was in error, and that she indeed did not have any entangling alliance.

I was due to make another one of my road trips into the north land, and I wanted to establish some rapport with Miss Griffith. She was reputedly the most able secretary in the office, and I was to learn it was a richly deserved reputation. But I knew no person acquainted with Miss Griffith who might make a formal introduction. I had met her shortly after my involvement in a minor auto collision with a Bureau vehicle, which required endless explanations regarding the accident. Connie took dictation for the ensuing reports. The more I saw of her the more I wanted to date her.

One day Connie was on the expedite desk, which was located in the same area in which the agents dictated their reports. Her desk was near the water fountain, and I found more than adequate reason for visiting the water fountain in the hope that my courage would hold up, and I might engage her in conversation. I asked her about where she grew up, went to college, and her previous work history. Finally I got around to asking if I could take her out that same night. Because of our age difference—I was nine years older—she had apparently not consid-

Connie Griffith at the Minneapolis office of the Federal Bureau of Investigation with a senior agent.

ered the possibility of a liaison with me. When I asked for a date she first stated she had promised a roommate they would go shopping together. I explained I was leaving the next day for a long road trip and might be gone several weeks, exaggerating a little bit. She finally agreed that she would shop with her friend and then meet me at the Dyckman Hotel lobby for dinner.

We soon found a mutual attraction with each other, I being more enthusiastic than she was. We had a delightful time getting acquainted and I swore I would be calling her.

The next day I departed for the north country, stopping for the night at Brainerd, Minnesota. After storing the Bureau car I went to have dinner and found myself thinking of her more and more intently. I decided to try to reach her by long distance but her roommate said she was out on a date, which was more than a little disappointing.

The next day while I was working in the Bemidji area, I called her again at about the same time in the evening only to find that she was on yet another date. All this did little for my ego, and I decided upon a course of action. I would find abundant reason the next day for returning to headquarters. But first I called Connie again and was met with a warmer reception. Returning to Minneapolis, I took Connie out to dinner. I came armed with a dozen long-stemmed red roses. At an appropriate time during the course of the evening, I said to her, "I know you'll think I'm crazy, but will you marry me?"

She was taken aback by a proposal so soon and evaded giving a definitive answer. But as things progressed, it became assumed that we would marry. Meanwhile I was awaiting orders to return to Washington for further training. The additional training may have been related to a rumor that I might be made a resident agent of a Bureau office in Aberdeen, South Dakota.

We were apart for two weeks, during which time I became more and more devoted to the idea of marriage to Connie. On my return from Washington, I was advised that I had indeed been moved to the Aberdeen position, which put some 200 miles between me and my beloved. Connie greeted this new development with disappointment.

The FBI Years **95**

One of our favorite places while we were dating was Jenning's, a large log cabin on the edge of town where we could have dinner and dance to live music. Once the manager asked Connie if she was 21, which was the minimum age for admission. Connie, who was then 19 but appeared to be much younger, asserted that she was 21. The manager asked me if I would sign an affidavit to that effect and present some identification. I pulled out by FBI credentials, and we were given the best table in the house, right in front of the fireplace. J. Edgar Hoover might not have approved of this.

Ultimately, after I was transferred to Aberdeen, I was able to see Connie only on weekends. All of this motivated me to find another career.

FBI agents and Connie in a meeting with a witness at the FBI office in Minneapolis.

Galveston and the Rackets

Jim and Connie on their wedding day in Sioux Falls in 1952.

A New Life and a Bride in Texas

After I decided to leave the FBI, I applied for a job with an older lawyer, Cecil Palmer, who had offices in the bank building in Dickinson, Texas. Lawyers were not in great demand, and my salary reflected this fact—I would be paid $150 a month. I had saved some money while in Chicago and Minneapolis, and Connie and I thought we could make it, albeit on meager rations, if Connie was able to work. I resigned from the FBI and returned to Texas in order to prepare for our life together as man and wife.

We resolved to marry on December 27, 1952. We had greater courage than good judgment. Actually, if there had been such a program as food stamps we would have been at the top of the eligibility list. While my pay was meager, it was not unfair because I had not yet developed marketable skills.

Connie came from a big family with big hearts. They welcomed me into the family and our wedding gifts filled my little 1952 model Ford. (It was my only worldly possession and I didn't owe a penny on it.) My wife had scrimped and saved and had paid back the loan she had taken out in order to have the one year of college she enjoyed at South Dakota State University.

Our honeymoon consisted of our journey from Sioux Falls to Dickinson. Upon arriving in Dickinson, Connie was favorably impressed with the beauty of the pine trees and the bayou. I had rented a small apartment in an old building previously known as the 75 Club, which had been a gambling joint. I left Connie to the unpacking while I went off to work, hoping to earn my keep. Connie looked out from the two story window of our apartment house and saw a drab field devoid of charm but equipped with a multitude of oil wells. Unless you own an oil well, its beauty is lost on you.

I had settled in a part of Texas where I had no relatives and

100 Flak Bait

Jim, Connie, and Connie's little sister, Carol, Easter 1952, in Sioux Falls, South Dakota.

few friends. I promptly addressed the problem of not being acquainted by trying to meet as many people as possible and to form a good impression in the hope of increasing our law practice. I was somewhat taken aback by the fact that the major industry of the Galveston County area seemed to be gambling and the associated rackets. I knew, of course, that gambling was illegal, and I immediately asked how it could exist alongside honest government. In discussing this matter I want to make clear I had no prudish notions about dictating how other folks spend their time or their money. I consider that a person's own business. However, when such endeavors rely on the corruption of state and local government, I then begin to ask questions.

The predominant view in the county was that gambling, prostitution, and illegal traffic in liquor were good for the local economy, and therefore these activities should be encouraged rather than prohibited. In my experience, I had been exposed to generally high standards prevalent in U.S. law enforcement. While the federal government had its imperfections, it at least would not tolerate open violation of the law.

At that time, I had very little knowledge of the existence of the organized crime organization known as the Maceo Syndicate. I may have been the only person in that part of Texas who didn't know about the Maceos, who controlled the organized crime that had flourished in Galveston County for many years. Gambling, prostitution, and other illegal activity represented a vast industry, estimated to employ more than 4,000 people. Its impact on the community was considerable, and it permeated everything from corner grocery stores to churches to local government.

The Maceo Syndicate was very conscious of its public image, and, consequently, constantly engaged in activity to support charitable causes and to appear to be good citizens of the community. In addition to providing a payroll for many persons, it was also a source of funding for such things as the United Way and a seamless web of social programs. Why then in the world would a person of sound mind be so bold as to suggest that society would be better served without the rackets? I was well aware that the slightest suggestion that the community would be better served without organized crime would be met with much contention, if not violence.

Many people believed that to oppose the rackets was to put one's life in serious jeopardy. As my wife Connie and I settled in to the community, I began to become acquainted with the conventional wisdom regarding this subject. It was plainly evident the gambling enterprises were systematically siphoning off the disposable income of a considerable part of Texas. Meanwhile, the influence on honest government was palpable. Any person thinking of seeking public office became immediately aware of the importance of having the support of the rackets. Somehow, this struck me as doing violence to the concept of a democratic society. Thomas Jefferson and others at the time of the founding of the Republic had spoken of a dream of a government of the people, by the people, and for the people. Instead we had become a government of the Maceos, by the Maceos, and for the Maceos.

As the owners and operators of the largest part of the criminal syndicate, the Maceos controlled the essential elements of state and local government. They could not operate without the complicity of government, because what they were doing was clearly illegal. So any person who aspired to serve as a member of the state legislature, as a judge, as district attorney, or in virtually any other capacity was required to first make peace with the powers that be. I must confess I was naive enough to be utterly shocked by such an arrangement. The fox was in charge of the chicken coop.

I had tried, in concert with others, to correct this unconscionable condition, but to no avail. We had formed a citizens' committee for law enforcement, seeking to reform state and local government. I spoke with fellow lawyers and prominent citizens, most of whom shook their heads in wonderment and, I suspect, privately questioned my sanity. Some would say if I didn't like conditions in Galveston then I should go back from whence I came.

The easier course would have seemed to adopt the policy, "To get along, go along" and follow the path of least resistance. After all, the people involved in the rackets and their adherents were not bothering me. Many of them on the surface appeared friendly and even encouraging, so why should I rock the boat? The answer lay in the fact that I could find no one else willing to disturb the status quo.

I spoke with several leaders of the legal profession who had had serious experience in the handling of major criminal cases. I offered my support if they were inclined to clean up the rackets by running for district attorney. (The job was then called county attorney, although it had the same prosecutorial function that we now associate with the role of district attorney.) However, the job of district attorney paid $6,500 a year, which would have meant a substantial pay cut for most established lawyers. Others were unwilling to face the resistance in the community that would confront a reform-minded prosecutor.

The path that duty seemed to dictate was not exactly what I had bargained for on becoming a lawyer. I had hoped merely to improve upon the skills gained in law school, and was quite content to earn a reasonable living for my family. I had never before considered running for public office. Indeed, when I announced for the office of chief prosecutor, I did so with much trepidation. Had I taken counsel of my fears, rather than of my hopes, I would never have run. In fact, just a few short days after I had made a speech in which I committed to enforcing the law, I suddenly had severe reservations about the wisdom of my course. There was no groundswell of demand that I undertake the sacrifices and dangers of opposing the powerful influence of the criminal syndicate. But I finally concluded that my conscience would allow me to take no other path.

The only thing left for me to do was to throw my own hat in the ring.

I knew that I would need to raise the funds for a hard fought campaign. Little did I know how difficult that would be. But in the spring of 1954, I went to the Galveston County Courthouse and filed as a candidate for district attorney.

Why I Opposed Organized Crime

Why, one may ask, did I feel compelled to declare war on those whom I believed were engaged in corrupting the law? The reasons for my belief are many and varied. How could one who believed in the rule of law sit idly by while there was one set of rules for organized criminals and another set for the average citizen? How could we continue to lecture young people on matters of responsibility, while we, ourselves, were abdicating our responsibility for honest government. Why, indeed!

I suppose that the path that had led me to Galveston prepared me for what I encountered there and shaped the way I responded to it. After all, I had come from a cotton patch in Coryell County, from three years in the Air Force, much of it spent in England, France, and aloft over Germany, and two years in the FBI in Washington, Chicago, and Minnesota.

The G.I. Bill of Rights had given me the opportunity and the hope for the first time in life to secure an education and perhaps to make some difference in the world around me. I came from modest means but I did obtain a good education, which had led me to possess a fundamental belief in the importance of honest government. My travels throughout America and in Europe exposed me to the world beyond the cotton patch. All this led me to become familiar with the history of our land and a grasp of the principles of self government. While stationed in Boston in the Army, I took it upon myself to journey out to Lexington and Concord and to become familiar with the place where the first shots of the Revolutionary War were exchanged.

I committed to memory the poem:

> By the rude bridge that arched the flood,
> Their flag to April's breeze unfurled,
> Here once the embattled farmers stood
> And fired the shot heard round the world.

To me this was a tremendous lesson. How could a group of farmers untrained in combat defy the most powerful empire on earth? What impelled these early Americans to shake off the ancient shackles and to seek a more perfect union? I had just arrived from the European continent aboard a liberty ship and had reached an important juncture in my young life. This real life experience, together with my studies at the University of Texas, combined to make me believe that I might somehow find a way to improve the state of our existence.

If the concepts of American history had sufficient merit that we would fight and die for them, then perhaps there was sufficient reason to fight for the belief in a free and open society. I was soon to learn that an idea standing alone was not self actuating. As one of my professors exclaimed, an idea will work only if someone of conviction and belief makes it work. When my ideas about honest law enforcement were rebuffed by prominent people, I found that I must either put up or shut up.

A few short years before the events described herein, I was actively engaged in America's role in the Second World War. I had witnessed young Americans performing countless acts of bravery in defense of the principles for which America had long stood.

Jefferson had taught us that our democracy was based on the consent of the governed. This had to be an informed consent of the governed. I felt that each generation, including my own, or perhaps especially my own, had an obligation to preserve, protect, and defend the concept of orderly government, based on the rule of law. I lived in a community where school children walked past gaming houses and houses of prostitution. How could children reared in such an atmosphere be expected to grow up to be productive and principled citizens? Constituted authority in my adopted county had proven time and again to be unworthy of trust in large part. Men who had taken an oath to enforce the law had become a part of the problem, and not a part of the solution.

So, in spite of my inexperience and lack of standing in the community, I set about the task of organizing a campaign, formulating a strategy, and fund raising. The latter was a heavy burden, and I knew that my opposition would be well funded by those deeply invested in preserving the status quo. Now it was time for me to persuade my fellow citizens to help me in this effort to establish honest government and to defend the rule of law in Galveston County.

The Campaign

Immediately upon announcing as a candidate for District Attorney, I made it clear that if I were elected, it would be my job to root out all the vestiges of illegal gambling and other illegal rackets. I seized upon every conceivable opportunity to make a public address on the subject of honesty in government. I told my listeners that most young men seeking public office proclaimed they sought office at the insistence of their many friends. I tried to be honest by acknowledging that I did not have very many friends and that the few I had thought I was crazy for trying to get elected by opposing the rackets. There probably were 4,000 eligible voters whose livelihoods depended on corrupt law enforcement, so advocating upholding the law cost me 4,000 votes from the start.

I scraped together enough money to buy 15 minutes of advertising time on the new television station KGUL in Galveston in order to state frankly my position on gambling and corruption. This was probably the first instance of employing television in local elections in the state of Texas. In those days, if an advertiser was willing to run the risk of altering the TV schedule to displace a previously scheduled program—potentially alienating the program's regular audience in the process—then a mere $120 could purchase a 15-minute TV segment on Channel 11. This would enable me to go into the living room of many homes throughout the county.

I placed ads in local newspapers announcing the date and

time I would be appearing on Channel 11 and used all other means to drum up a large viewing audience. At the very outset I candidly stated my attitude about the need to destroy the criminal syndicate in Galveston County. Furthermore, I announced that my wife was at home beside the TV set (one which I was required to rent since I didn't even own a TV set) and that she would receive calls of those willing to contribute financially or otherwise to my campaign. Not a solitary person called to offer even so much as moral support. My experiment in political advertising was met with thundering silence.

Back to square one. I now became devoted to what is known as a "shoe leather campaign." I was young and energetic, and I could and did campaign for as long as 18 hours a day. I vowed

Jim and Connie at Jim's parents' home in Temple.

this race would not be lost by a lack of effort on my part. Soon I did see some signs of encouragement. However, often I would hear: "Jim, I know you are right and things are bad, and I want to help you, but please don't let anybody else know." I confess that to this day I don't know how a citizen could be of help by keeping their support a deep, dark secret.

Many of the unions endorsed my efforts, and I had considerable support among the members of the University of Texas Medical Branch community. I had four opponents, virtually all of whom had greater experience than I had. I was at a further disadvantage because I had resided in the county only 18 months at the time of the primary in July 1954. At least one of my opponents, Jules Damiani, Jr., had extensive experience as a prosecutor and was fundamentally a good man. However, he publicly stated that he would not disturb the status quo in terms of the rackets.

During the campaign my wife and friends feared for my safety. Connie insisted that I look under the hood of the car each morning and take other precautions. Members of the rackets had the nerve to attend some of the open air political rallies to show their opposition to me. At Walter Hall Park in League City, a group of them parked their cars and a pickup truck directly in front of the speaker's podium in an attempt to intimidate me. I turned it to my advantage by pointing them out, calling their names, and predicting that they would have a place reserved for them in the state penitentiary if I got elected. They didn't seem to enjoy the recognition.

I discounted notions that my life was in danger because I felt that if the racketeers killed a young former FBI agent, husband, father, and candidate for public office, the aftermath of such an assassination would spell the death knell for all the rackets in Galveston. I presumed that the racketeers had the intelligence to realize this as well.

However, only the month before the primary, on June 18, 1953, the Democratic candidate for attorney general of the State of Alabama was shot to death while leaving his law office in Phenix City, Alabama. Phenix City was infamous for gambling, prostitution, and corrupt government, and the candidate, Albert Patterson, had made cleaning up the city his primary campaign promise.

I was probably afforded a certain amount of protection by the fact that some racketeers themselves were spreading the rumor that I was still an FBI agent, and that J. Edgar Hoover had planted me here to bring about changes over which the FBI then had no jurisdiction. An assassination under these circumstances would have been even more ominous for the syndicate.

The endless campaigning soon became exhausting. The issue was so divisive that oftentimes contact with members of the public became explosive. The issue was further complicated by the widely held belief that the rackets were helpful to the welfare of the county through their philanthropic gestures. Some suggested that the United Fund could not succeed without the support of the racketeers. The criminal element waged this sort of public relations effort year round with no one refuting the claim that the rackets were good for the economy and for charity. Of course, the rackets extracted millions of dollars more from the economy than they contributed to charity, and all of the illegal income escaped taxes. This situation so emboldened corrupt officials that it infected local government at every level.

For example, on Galveston Island the Police and Fire Commissioner was traditionally a lawyer. While serving as Police Commissioner, Walter Johnston decided he would act as defense counsel in a murder case. Of course, the murder investigation was conducted by his employees and his role as defense counsel was at cross purposes to the work of his own department, a clear case of conflict of interest. He was in a position to influence both sides of the case, even to the point of inhibiting the police investigation to the benefit of the criminal client who was paying his fee. It did not require a brilliant legal analysis to determine that this was improper.

I contacted the Galveston County Bar Association, and after much haranguing, the police commissioner agreed to step down as counsel for the defense.

I became alternately hopeful and depressed over the

prospects we faced. It became more and more difficult to attract campaign funds, and I had about reached the limits of my borrowing capacity. I remarked to friends that I was convinced the winner would simply be the last survivor.

With five men in the race it was considered unlikely any one of us would secure a majority of the votes in the first primary. Friends said they had given up on the hope of winning—their only hope was that I might survive to reach the runoff. When

Connie and Jim at a Democratic fundraiser at the home of Walter Hall, League City.

election results were finally tallied, I shocked the underworld and the community by corralling more votes than any opponent. Indeed I was 1,010 votes over my nearest opponent. Once again I went to the public stating that victory was within our grasp, but that I needed campaign funds. The response was not much greater than my earlier efforts. I needed to harness all my energy for the month ahead. The runoff election was scheduled to be held in 30 days.

A Bribe Offered

I resorted again to a shoe leather campaign. I met workers at the refinery gates as they appeared for work early in the morning, I campaigned hand to hand at supermarkets, and I walked door to door in neighborhoods. At one point I became so discouraged at my efforts to win votes on the island that I felt like giving up, but I could not bring myself to quit. So I pressed on, campaigning throughout the county with special emphasis on the mainland, where I had done extremely well in the primary.

I knew the rackets must have begun to feel some fear about the election and that we could expect desperate efforts to defeat me. It came in an interesting form. I had an older brother, almost a father to me, named Dick Simpson. Dick had devoted his life to working in the oil industry as a roustabout, roughneck, and driller. Dick had an old friend residing in Houston who had become quite wealthy in the pipe wrapping business, which became prominent with the advent of the Big Inch and Little Inch pipelines carrying oil to the northeast. His name was John Rosson. I had met John when he and Dick flew to Austin shortly before my graduation from the UT Law School. They came in Rosson's private airplane, and they took me to dinner at which my brother gave me a handsome gold-plated Bulova watch for graduation.

It turned out that Rosson, an entirely legitimate businessman, had engaged in the practice of bringing potential clients down to Galveston County to gamble at crap tables and roulette wheels. One night at one of the clubs in Dickinson, Rosson overheard some gamblers denouncing me and saying they believed they could defeat me at the polls but that meanwhile I was giving them a lot of bad press. He overheard them call my name and innocently said to them, "I know a fellow named Jack Simpson who is a brother of the dearest friend I have on earth, Dick Simpson." The gamblers immediately seized on this connection in the interest of getting me out of the race and ending the bad publicity that was being generated by the election.

One of the racketeers asked if Rossen would speak to his friend, my brother Dick, to point out the error of my ways and offer me a bribe to withdraw. The gamblers sent word through Dick that they would pay me $30,000 to drop out of the race. I want to make clear that neither my brother nor John Rosson did anything unethical or illegal.

With some reluctance my brother agreed to speak to me without urging me to take action one way or another.

Dick called me at my home in Dickinson to say he would like to talk with me. He and I were of a very close family, he being the oldest son, me the youngest. In our meeting he simply laid out the proposal of the rackets by the terms of which I would be paid $30,000 in cash upon announcing that I was withdrawing from the race. As soon as Dick finished talking I immediately said, "Dick, you know I'm not going to do that." He made no effort at all to persuade me but instead went back to see the gambler who had instigated the effort. Dick told him in no uncertain terms that I had declined the offer. Whereupon the gambler said something to the effect of, "I am sure you know I cannot be responsible for what may happen now." Of course, this was a veiled threat against me.

My brother, who was tougher than nails, said, "Oh yes, you will be responsible in the event anything happens to my baby brother. If you so much as harm one hair on his head, I will come back to this county. One night you will park your car in the garage, and the last sound you will hear will be my .45 going off in your ear. Is that plain enough?" The gambler acknowledged that Dick had made his point, and they parted company. Dick returned to my home and related all of this to me.

At that moment I knew that the rackets considered me a threat to win.

The Runoff

By leading the entire pack in the primary I immediately became the target in more ways than one. I was shaking the roots of the illegal empire to its very foundation and it required little imagination to discern that millions of dollars were at stake. I did little to defuse this situation. My campaign rhetoric became more and more clear-cut. Corruption had undermined democratic government in Galveston County and I intended to put a stop to it.

I had a good friend at the time who was a career FBI agent and serving as the resident agent of the FBI for Galveston County. John Franklin was old enough to be my father and in some ways he looked upon me as a son. Occasionally he would call and insist that we go for a walk in the parts of town dominated by gambling enterprises. I pointed out to him that he courted some danger for himself and his career by imparting a mantle of protection over me in this way. He discounted the danger and insisted that the very purpose of our walks was to deliver a message to the racketeers that an attack on me would be considered an attack on him and the Federal Bureau of Investigation. It should be noted that at that time, the FBI had no jurisdiction over the types of crime that I promised to end if I were elected.

Johnny Franklin thought I should go to the very top of the power structure of Galveston and meet with Colonel W. L. Moody, the patriarch of a banking, insurance, and real estate empire that included American National Insurance and Moody National Bank. Colonel Moody had never had an open break with the Maceos, but it was always possible that the equation had changed with my strong showing in the primary. If he agreed with my views perhaps he might even help fund my runoff effort. An appointment was made for me to sit down and talk with Colonel Moody. We met in his offices in the American National Insurance building. He was cordial enough, but it soon became apparent that we were not destined to join forces. The most I got out of him was a promise that if he were in town on the runoff date he would give some thought to voting for me. I realized I had struck out completely.

I returned to traditional campaigning. Most people in business were afraid of their shadow and did not want to be seen in my presence. Other lawyers, even close friends, shunned me as if I had the plague. This takes a toll on the human psyche. I tended to campaign more on the mainland because it was there that I received the warmest reception. Occasionally I would be shocked to find opposition and hostility where I had every right to expect warm support. For example, I had represented a widow whose husband died while still serving on the Galveston Police Department. His monthly salary of $250 was an indicator of the low regard the power structure had for honest government. The city refused to pay the unused sick leave that the officer, whose surname was Hime, had accrued. Efforts to settle this dispute were met with stonewalling. The case proceeded to trial before a distinguished and thoroughly honest District Judge, Charles G. Dibrell, Sr., who happened to disagree with my interpretation of the rights of the widow to receive unused sick leave benefits. The trial judge ruled against us, and I appealed to the Court of Appeals, never charging the widow a fee. The three-judge Court of Appeals ruled unanimously in my favor, and I collected the benefits. The court ordered that the city pay my fee. It was a complete victory for the widow, and my services had cost her nothing, so I felt this would be one Galveston family standing beside me during the runoff.

Imagine my disbelief of seeing my opponent's bumper

sticker on the car of the widow's son. I was later to learn that this incident alone might have determined the outcome of the race.

As we moved closer to the finish line, the battle lines became clear. *The Galveston Daily News* opposed me in its editorials and endorsed my runoff opponent, referring to me as a "Johnny Come Lately." The Maceo Empire published its own slate card on which my runoff opponent was endorsed.

Connie and Jim about 1955.

I was disappointed that the Galveston County Bar Association, my own professional colleagues, refused to take any stand. And the bar was joined by the medical profession in remaining neutral, in spite of the heavy toll that prostitution, gambling, and illegal alcohol took on public health and the lives of individuals and families.

I knew the race would conclude with a razor sharp margin, but I could not believe that the difference between victory and defeat was a mere eight votes. I still remember the exact vote count. It was 12,280 votes for Marsene Johnson and 12,272 votes for me. As I grappled with the loss I was reminded of a comment by Abraham Lincoln. When a young lad stubbed his toe, Lincoln recounted, the boy said that he was too old to cry and it hurt too much to laugh.

Now came the task of putting the pieces of our lives back together again. I was overdrawn in both my personal bank account and my campaign account. I couldn't help but wonder if the whole endeavor was worth the effort when the public responded with such complacency. The only thing left was to resolve that we would be alert to any opportunities in the future to strike a blow for honest government. But I resolved that it would have to come without my name on the ballot.

After Defeat— the Beginning of the End

To say I was disappointed at losing by the razor thin margin of eight votes would be an understatement. Someone once observed that victory has many fathers, but that defeat is a bastard. Few people called me to express their sadness at such a narrow loss. Strangely enough, however, there were several people who felt compelled to call with spiteful messages such as: "That will teach you to mind your own business! If you don't like the way things are here, why in hell don't you go back to where you came from?" I had seldom seen such animosity expressed by so many people.

As for myself, I was content with the campaign I had waged. I never wavered in my principles, and I persevered in the face of adversity throughout the race. Before the campaign, I said to myself that I was the only person in Galveston County who believed in victory. But I had demonstrated that half of the people of the county were in favor of change. That was no small achievement.

By now, the newest member of the Simpson clan, my daughter Simone, was almost two years of age. I had the responsibility of a wife and daughter, and few resources with which to support them. Fortunately, I had a profession and a place to hang my hat. The folks beating the path to my law office were few in number, but I set about the task of sharpening my skills as a lawyer and developing a practice.

A few weeks after the campaign, my spirits were lifted by a phone call from Owen Barker, who himself had fought the criminal underworld as a young district attorney a generation before me. He was one of the most respected lawyers in the county and a real prince of a fellow. His offices were in Galveston with his son, Jerry D. Barker. Jerry and I had been classmates at the University of Texas School of Law. To my great surprise—and great joy—their offer was to form the firm of Barker, Barker & Simpson. I was greatly flattered to be extended a partnership at the outset. I worried no small amount that I might not carry my part of the load in attracting clients and generating fees.

My partners thought that with my experience as an FBI agent, I might become proficient in both criminal and civil law. Like most young lawyers, I approached the task of establishing a law practice with trepidation. On the first day in the new office my fears were somewhat mitigated when I was hired to represent two brothers charged with a criminal offense in Brazoria County. I don't recall the amount of the fee I established, but I well remember that I quoted a retainer of $1,000 for accepting the case. Much to my surprise the young men came up with the retainer. I was pleased to report to Owen and Jerry that I had taken in $1,000 in cash. This may have reassured them that their new partner might be able to pull his weight after all.

In the process of running a county-wide race, I had gained some visibility and was now fairly well known throughout Galveston County. The press asked me if I would run again for district attorney. I concluded that, at this point, I owed more to my wife and child than I did to the cause. But I kept my foot in the door, never saying never. I vowed to myself that I would keep a sharp lookout for other ways of attacking organized crime.

I decided that out of respect for my senior partner, I should reach our law office before he arrived and never leave at the end of the day until after his departure. On one of the first days in the office I reported before opening time, and I found a young fellow about my age dressed in a business suit and asking to see me. I recall thinking that this was probably an insurance adjuster who might wish to settle one of my cases. After he was seated, I offered him a cup of coffee and inquired the reason for his visit. He said, "Mr. Simpson, I am here to talk with you about your retirement program." Little did he know how futile his visit would be, because I faced abundant demands on my meager financial resources. My immediate concern was putting bread on the table at home and fulfilling my obligation as a partner at the law firm. At this time I was still overdrawn in my bank account, and I still confronted unpaid bills from the campaign.

With the passage of time, I found greater and greater joy in my marriage and in my role as husband and father. Little did I know my baby girl would grow up to finish the same law school that I attended and to practice law with me.

While I decided not to run again for district attorney, I did remain politically active. During the next election, I noticed in the press a continuing story about a young district attorney who had destroyed the criminal empire of Dallas County and who was now seeking the office of attorney general of the State of Texas. He spoke emphatically about enforcing the law and holding public officials accountable for their misdeeds. His name was Will Wilson, an established lawyer and a combat veteran of the war in the Pacific. I had found my role model.

When Mr. Wilson was elected, I was elated. I immediately wrote a letter to the new attorney general-elect offering my congratulations and expressing my hope that he could fulfill his campaign pledge to shut down illegal enterprises in the state. I made reference to my own failed efforts, and I offered whatever assistance I could. Wilson did not write me back, but called on the telephone—even before he was sworn into office. He asked if I might come to Austin to discuss the state of law enforcement with him. Of course I could find the time to confer with the new attorney general.

At our meeting in Austin I discussed the situation in Galveston and outlined the legal approach I would recommend.

Special Assistant Attorney General Jim Simpson during the organized crime investigations in Galveston County, 1957. Photo by The Texas Observer.

I proposed using civil injunctions to shut down the rackets rather than criminal prosecutions. The civil injunction route has been seldom used, but it possesses several advantages. First, the burden of proof is much lighter. You don't have to prove your case beyond a reasonable doubt. Instead, you have to show by a preponderance of evidence that the accused is guilty of a crime. This makes good sense because you are not asking the court to send the defendant to jail, as in a criminal prosecution. In the case of an injunction, the prosecutor is asking the court to rebuke the defendant and enjoin him from further illegal activity. So it's easier to obtain a civil injunction than a criminal conviction. Second, the civil injunction does not require the cooperation of law enforcement officials. Because the police, the sheriff, and the local officials were all corrupt, any crackdown that depended on the assistance of law enforcement was doomed to failure. The only cooperation we would need in order to obtain the civil injunctions was an honest district judge. I knew we could depend on two: William E. Stone of the 56th District Court and Donald Markle of the 10th District Court.

However, I explained that this tactic would involve some expense. Wilson explained that during his term as district attorney of Dallas County, a wealthy businessman had long admired his work in cleaning up government. Wilson said that the businessman had offered funds for any project that the attorney general felt appropriate, so long as it advanced the cause of honest government. Wilson committed these funds to the investigation. The only condition was that the identity of the donor not be revealed so long as the donor was still living. I never learned the identity of the businessman, and I suspect that Will Wilson took that secret to his grave.

At this time, the attorney general offered me a job as special assistant attorney general, which I accepted.

My plan was to choose two men with or without prior law enforcement experience and then train them to carry out investigations against every business in flagrant violation of state law in Galveston County. I asked Wilson to trust my judgment regarding whom to hire as investigators. We could not pay the investigators, lest we run the risk of exposing them. Having practiced law in the community for five years, I had a wide range of acquaintances, and this, together with my time as an FBI agent, gave me a fairly good grasp of the type of person who could be trusted. I was then legal counsel for Local 449 of the Oil, Chemical and Atomic Workers International Union, which represented the employees of several Texas City plants.

First, I chose James D. ("Buddy") Givens, a clean cut and politically active refinery worker who had once mentioned in conversation that he thought that gambling drained money out of the legitimate economy. He had correctly pointed out that money that could have been used by his co-workers for food and clothing for their young children was instead going to racketeers and to pay bribes throughout government. Givens, 33, was diplomatic, discreet, and well-spoken, even though, like most refinery workers, he did not have much formal education. I explained to him this task would require some degree of danger, long hours, secrecy, and that once his identity was revealed, he would incur the wrath of a large number of people. He agreed without hesitation.

I then told him my criteria for selecting him and asked that he use the same yardstick in choosing a partner who would be known only to him and to me until the investigation was complete and the crackdown had occurred. Meanwhile, Givens and his partner would work under my control and direction. My FBI experience in planning, carrying out, and reporting investigations proved valuable to our effort.

Buddy Givens knew a man who could be trusted and was suited to the assignment. He outlined the nature of the task to Carroll Yaws, 37, a fellow worker at the American Oil Company refinery in Texas City. Givens and Yaws were close friends and confidants. When Buddy brought Carroll Yaws to me for my approval, I was immediately impressed. Both men were perfect for the job.

I did tell them that after the investigation had run its course, I would try to get them some form of compensation, but I could not promise that I would succeed. It would not have been a

122   Flak Bait

tempting offer to someone who was just involved for the money. However, we did have Attorney General Wilson's special account from which we could compensate the men for their expenses, which were recorded in great detail.

Givens and Yaws worked in tandem and made their trips to gambling joints and illegal enterprises without me. It's hard to imagine such an important task being undertaken by civilian volunteers today, but we had no choice since organized crime had so thoroughly corrupted the investigatory arms of government.

I suggested that the two men avoid telephone conversations and that we meet every few days to discuss how things were

The investigators: Refinery workers Carroll S. Yaws, 37, and James D. "Buddy" Givens, 33, with Jim Simpson, 33 (center). Photo by The Texas Observer.

going. Of course, finding illegal enterprises required no effort — the racketeer's operations were all hidden in plain sight. You couldn't go into a corner store or restaurant in Galveston without encountering slot machines. And the downtown gambling houses were a couple of blocks from the courthouse. I instructed Givens and Yaws to take highly detailed notes and to be careful in protecting such evidence of the investigation.

The two men, while engaged in illegal activities, would occasionally encounter people they knew. Because Givens was president of the Galveston County Young Democrats and both men had reputations as upstanding citizens, this could become embarrassing. Nevertheless, they behaved with great circumspection and kept meticulous records of what they observed. Our rule of thumb was for Givens and Yaws to make a minimum of four visits to each enterprise under investigation, meanwhile recording a full account of the illegal activity taking place, as well as their own illegal acts, such as buying liquor and gambling. We didn't ask them to obtain direct evidence at the bordellos, and I'm sure their wives would have concurred with that decision.

They started with mid-level racket joints. At a small gambling operation in Kemah, they happened to flash a roll of bills which caught the eye of a man who inquired, "Would you men like to go for some real high stakes gambling?" With their hearts in their throats they accepted his invitation. The man instructed them to follow him in their car to a palatial residence on Galveston Bay. Upon entering, the men determined that it was a high-dollar gambling house. Suddenly, it occurred to Buddy Givens that he had left his notes from several nights of investigations in the glove compartment of his car, which was unlocked and under the care of an employee of the gambling operation. He made a plausible excuse for returning to his car. With his heart pounding like a drum, he retrieved the precious cache of records. Realizing that if his notes had fallen into the wrong hands he might become more intimately familiar with the marine life of Galveston Bay, Givens vowed to be more careful in the future.

The Isle of Vice

During much of the 20th century, Galveston was known as the Isle of Vice, and it earned its reputation. One health agency, the American Social Hygiene Association (ASHA), reported that Galveston was home to more prostitutes per capita than any other city in the nation. Indeed, the ASHA was thrilled to learn that Attorney General Will Wilson was serious about eliminating the island's prostitution rackets.

So far as I could determine, Galveston was the only city in America in which the elected mayor was an open advocate in favor of organized prostitution. It requires little stretch of the imagination to discern the connection between organized prostitution and corruption of government. Prostitution involves large amounts of cash, some of which get diverted to law enforcement officers and public officials in return for protection.

Among the many colorful houses of prostitution, perhaps the most infamous was the Bristol Hotel. In our investigations, the court records suggested that the owner of the Bristol Hotel was First Hutchings Sealy National Bank. Even for Galveston, this was shocking news. First Hutchings Sealy National Bank was a well-established bank on the island, founded by some of the city's oldest families. It catered to the carriage trade, and few of its customers would expect the distinguished bank and its officers to be operating a whorehouse.

In order to prove title we issued a subpoena for the bank's records and, lo and behold, our suspicions were confirmed. First Hutchings Sealy was in the bordello business. At the same time, we subpoenaed the bank officer who was custodian of record of the Bristol. He was sworn in and placed on the stand to answer my questions about the relationship between the bank and the bawdy house. Questioning was along these lines:

"Are you Tom Lane?"

Answer: "Yes."

"Tell the Court your job."

Answer: "I am the custodian of records showing the bank ownership of certain real estate."

"Do those records reflect that the bank owns the Bristol Hotel?"

Answer: "Yes, sir."

"Mr. Lane, were the folks at the staid First Hutchings Sealy National Bank aware the Bristol Hotel was operated as a house of ill repute?"

Answer: "Counsel, let me put it this way. We knew the Bristol was not exactly the Waldorf Astoria, but we really didn't know it was a whorehouse."

By the time the court room laughter subsided, the judge, the venerable Donald Markle, ended the Bristol Hotel's days as a house of prostitution with the stroke of his pen. The judge signed civil injunctions compelling the illegal operations to cease or be held in contempt of court.

I found it amusing that Galveston then engaged in a debate over the question of whether or not organized prostitution was desirable in the community. Strangely enough, the most eloquent and strongest advocate of prostitution was the elected mayor, Herbert Cartwright. The mayor was very personable and people liked him. He was a fairly recent graduate of the University of Texas, and he opposed those of us he deemed as "do-gooders." At the height of his popularity, he issued a challenge to debate state representative Bill Kugle, who opposed prostitution and other illegal vices. Kugle, also a graduate of UT, had fought in the Second World War as a paratrooper and had earned a Purple Heart for wounds received in combat. One might think his superb war record would have provided adequate defense against those in the community who sought to attack Kugle and defend organized crime and corruption. Nevertheless, Kugle was viewed by many as an interloper and troublemaker. Bill Kugle was an honor graduate of the University of Texas School of Law and a skilled debater, so he was a worthy opponent in the debate.

The Junior Chamber of Commerce had agreed to sponsor the event. Ironically, it was scheduled to be held at the

Hollywood Dinner Club, a casino and restaurant that was now padlocked by injunction. The Hollywood had been enjoined by a district court order from continued use as a place of illegal activity. The date and place of the debate had been agreed upon, but as the time grew nearer, reason seemed to take hold in the mind of the mayor, as he found a convenient reason why he could not appear for the event. The gambling interests had determined that it would be counterproductive to provide a powerful speaker like Kugle with a forum at which his rhetoric might crush Mayor Cartwright in debate and build support for reform. So, despite a considerable crowd having gathered, it was announced the debate would not occur. It was one of the few instances in which a spokesman for the racketeers was subjected to ridicule.

The Balinese Room and the Texas Rangers

Once we had investigated the smaller gambling venues on the mainland, we were ready to approach the larger and more-celebrated casinos on Galveston Island. The investigators and I, as well as the Attorney General in Austin, were anxious to complete the investigation of the fabled Balinese Room, which was the flagship of the Maceo empire. The Balinese Room was located on a pier jutting out into the Gulf of Mexico, some 200 yards from the Galveston seawall.

Peggy Lee, Jimmy Dorsey, Phil Harris, and Freddy Martin performed at the Balinese Room, where Houston oilmen such as Diamond Jim West and Glenn McCarthy, not to mention Houston Mayor Louie Welch, were regulars. So popular was the Balinese Room that when I had sought election as district attorney a few years earlier, a number of highly placed individuals offered support under the condition that I promise never to bother the Balinese Room. I found this proposal highly offensive and so told them.

I briefed the attorney general on the preparations we had made for shutting down the Balinese Room, and he approved the plan of attack. Next on the agenda was a larger raid to close all the gambling joints in Galveston County. Wilson had a good friend named James Nowell who had office space available in Houston for planning the big raid. Secrecy was of the utmost importance. I had warned the group that it was hard to keep a secret when a large number of persons, with deeply vested interests, were affected. In fact, I insisted that my own wife Connie should prepare the crucial paperwork. She worked on the search warrants and the injunctions that were at the heart of our work. This tiny 97-pound woman greeted a host of law enforcement officers at our residence in Texas City, where she not only prepared the crucial documents, but served cookies and coffee for everyone. Big hats literally filled our little house on 24th Avenue North in Texas City.

In my earliest meetings with Attorney General Wilson, I sought to stress with him my views of the problems in gaining the cooperation of other law enforcement agencies. I had very reluctantly come to the view that the Texas Rangers could not be counted upon in the fight against Galveston County racketeers. This view was difficult for me to embrace because I had grown up in central Texas admiring the Rangers. As a lad, I had read the famed book by Walter Prescott Webb, *The Texas Rangers*, which conveyed the notion that the Rangers were men of great courage and integrity. I hesitate to mention these facts, but this account would not be accurate without an honest and truthful presentation of the problem posed by vast sums of money flowing through illegal channels. Gambling alone is harmful enough to be outlawed, but the way gambling was conducted in many Texas counties led to the inevitable corruption of local law enforcement. I suggested to the attorney general that, if possible, we should omit the Rangers entirely from our plans. The Rangers were known for staging cosmetic raids, appearing to shut down the rackets; however, in a few weeks they were back

Connie Griffith Simpson typing the injunction suits at her home in Texas City, 1957. Regular law enforcement offices in Galveston County could not be trusted with the information. Photo by The Texas Observer.

Galveston and the Rackets 129

in full operation. After all, the Rangers had had the authority to shut down the rackets for decades. In those days, a person could be charged with vagrancy just for being near a place of gambling, prostitution, or other illegal activity. No warrant was needed to pick up the racketeers and their customers and throw them in jail. The Texas Rangers could have ended gambling, prostitution, and the illegal sale of alcohol by rounding up the operators and their customers a few times. Once people realized that a visitor to the Turf Club, the Rodeo Club, or the Balinese Room might end the evening behind bars, the rackets would have been forced to close.

Jim reading injunction petitions after a long night of legal work, 1957.

130   Flak Bait

We had every reason to believe, and I remain convinced, that the Rangers were paid off. John Klevenhagen, a captain of the Texas Rangers, was always openly hostile to me. Our actions were shutting off the flow of bribes and posed a threat to the corrupt status quo.

Stories abounded about the famed Balinese Room. There was a guard station at the head of the pier, equipped with an alarm that would inform the gamblers that a raid was in progress. During the time it took to walk from the seawall to the gaming rooms over the Gulf, the slot machines could be folded up into the walls and the craps tables transformed into an innocent game of backgammon. In earlier raids, by the time the Rangers reached the gaming rooms, the gambling devices were cleverly stored away and the orchestra would begin to play, "The Eyes of Texas." A few arrests might be made, but within days business continued as usual.

Earlier in 1957, a runaway grand jury had indicted some 22 members of the rackets, including Sam and Rose Maceo, on gambling charges. Speculation was rampant that the local prosecutor would dismiss the indictments of such powerful men. And in fact, he did! The local state representative, Bill Kugle, branded this action as an insult to every law abiding citizen of Texas.

Kugle's statement inspired outrage in Galveston, as well as his political demise at the polls a few months later. Bill Kugle was a man of courage who had served as a paratrooper in World War II. The local prosecutor who requested the dismissal of the gambling indictments soon announced his candidacy for district judge. Not only was he not chastised for his dereliction of duty, but he felt he had earned a promotion!

Once we began to focus on the island, we prepared a two-pronged attack on the rackets. First, we would carry out a raid on the flagship Balinese Room, followed by raids on the Turf Club, the Western Room, the Rod and Gun Club, and scores of other gambling establishments and dozens of houses of prostitution. Second, we would seek injunctive relief through the district courts to enjoin the businesses from their illegal operations.

Attorney General Wilson remained confident that the Rangers would not betray our intentions. He once told me he could not believe that the Texas Rangers, who were sworn to enforce the law, would in fact betray the law.

The raid went forward as planned. The raiding party consisted of Texas Department of Public Safety troopers, the Texas Rangers, and an assistant attorney general. This caravan of law enforcement officers would be led down the Gulf Freeway in a car commanded by Homer Garrison, Director of the Department of Public Safety and chief of the Texas Rangers. I held my breath fearing the worst. Sure enough, when the raiding force reached the Balinese Room the gaming devices had all been moved and the place was as empty as a tomb.

My worst fears had been realized. Wilson was deeply disappointed, but I stressed that the failure of the raid did not undermine the validity of the suits for injunction. Obviously, the racketeers had received a tip on the impending raid. It was time now for Wilson's assistants to go to the district courts with petitions for injunctions in hand. Our two witnesses were on standby, and as each injunction suit was filed, they came forward to verify the truth of the allegations, thus placing the matter completely in the hands of the district judges.

On the first day of the filing, June 10, 1957, forty-seven separate injunctions were sought and obtained. These included the offenses of gaming, prostitution, and liquor violations.

Needless to say, the massive filing of injunction suits created more than a little flurry. Yet this was just the tip of the iceberg. Many more were to follow. At first many of the racketeers decided to dig in their heels and run the risk of being jailed for contempt of court. Just as promptly we moved with filing petitions seeking the incarceration of those who defied the court's injunctions. The violators were warned to bring their toothbrushes, because it was our intention to throw the violators in jail to teach them a lesson. Many were stunned because they had successfully evaded the long arm of the law for decades, but this was judgment day.

The defendants in these civil suits could require a hearing, but we had prepared an abundance of evidence to support our cases. I was confident that in the Balinese Room debacle, we had lost a battle but had won the war.

I remain convinced that the civil injunction strategy was crucial to our success. The investigations needed to be performed in secrecy and with great economy, and the injunctive approach could achieve both goals. Our burden was to show the court that at the target locations there was a pattern of conduct in clear defiance of the law. The burden of proof lay upon the State, but given the brazen manner in which these establishments engaged in criminal activity, this was not a difficult standard to meet. We had been careful during the investigative stage to keep meticulous records showing the dates, times, and locations of gambling practices and prostitution.

We were required to file a sworn petition accompanied by specific affidavits proving the allegations that supported the injunction. If we were successful, a temporary restraining order could be granted to ban the defendants from further illegal activity—even without giving notice to them. The defendants then had an opportunity within 10 days to show why the restraining order was improperly granted.

The businesses named in the civil injunctions are evocative of the era: the Western Room, the Stork Club, Moulin Rouge, the Mint Club, the Idle Hour Club, the Anchor Club, the Howl Club, the Bandbox, Ace Rooms, the Esquire, the Metropole, the Imperial Club, the Reno, Club 88 Keys, the Rickshaw Room, the Hurricane Club, Acme Rooms, Cozy Rooms, the Bamboo Club, The Palace, and of course, the Balinese Room.

The injunctions were important because if the defendants or their employees violated the terms of the court's order, they could be arrested and jailed immediately. This could be accomplished without a jury trial.

It would be difficult to state precisely how many individual injunctions were granted or how many individual citizens were enjoined. But a fair estimate would be close to 200, which is an indicator of how pervasive the criminal underworld had become.

How, one may ask, could things have gotten so far out of control that law abiding citizens had abandoned all hope of fair and equitable law enforcement? The conventional wisdom held that no district judge would sign an order terminating illegal conduct in Galveston County and that no jury would convict a person charged with participating in a criminal conspiracy. But once we were able to close down businesses that engaged in illegal activity, the racketeers were cut off from their cash flow. They could no longer afford to operate, much less to bribe law enforcement and public officials.

Finally people came to believe that this was one effort that might succeed. The usual stunt of waiting a few days and then resuming the criminal activity did not prevail. The attention focused on this effort generated some citizen involvement. One day, in the office we maintained in the Merimax Building, we received an informant's tip to the effect that a large cache of slot machines was located in the old Hollywood Dinner Club. The club had been closed years earlier. We swiftly obtained a search warrant, and lo and behold, we discovered some 2,000 slot machines, many of which were in their original crates. A few years earlier a young state senator, George Nokes of Navarro County, had secured the passage of a bill making the mere possession of a slot machine a felony. Accordingly, seizure of the illegal slots followed as a matter of law. We were free to dispose of the 2,000 slot machines however we pleased.

A giant bonfire was started, and many slot machines were broken to pieces by axe-wielding police officers and burned. However, the huge number of slot machines rendered the task overwhelming. A news reporter in Houston who occasionally contributed to *Life* magazine approached me with an idea for a photo opportunity. Why not put the slot machines on a barge and hurl them into Galveston Bay? The reporter would see that the resulting photo, showing the young Texas attorney general kicking the contraband into the bay, would appear in *Life*. This sounded too good to pass up. So I proceeded to the docks where I found a barge operator willing to let out his barge for a fee, which I promptly paid. Will Wilson came from Austin to be photographed administering the *coup de grace* to the slot machines in a scene full of symbolism. We chose a place near the old deserted concrete ship, a partially submerged vessel off Pelican Island. *Life* magazine never showed up after all, although newspapers all over Texas covered this event. While it was designed as a publicity stunt, the dumping of all those machines sent an important message that change was afoot in Galveston County.

The episode did not end there, however. The next day, a colonel in the Army Corps of Engineers called me to report that some of the slot machines had floated to the surface. A number of the shrimp boat operators complained that the floating slot machines posed a threat to navigation. I went to meet the colonel the next day and explained that we had indeed dumped the slots into the water. The colonel scolded me and ordered me to stop using the ship channel as a repository for slot machines. He advised me that the Corps of Engineers is charged with regulating waterborne interstate commerce and that it is illegal to impede navigation of regulated waterways. The gamblers in Galveston took great delight in the fact that I had been accused of violating the law.

Curiously, during the 1990s, I received a call from a professor at Rice University who asked that I accompany him on a boat to help locate the slot machines by means of sophisticated sonar equipment. I showed him where I threw the machines from a barge 40 years earlier. The professor's equipment indicated that the machines were still there on the bottom of the bay, where they remain to this day.

One of the more colorful characters of the period was the city recorder, Eddie Jahn, whose job was akin to a municipal judge and who was responsible for such matters as traffic violations. He was handsome, gregarious, and likeable. Jahn ran for judge in the 1940s against Judge Donald Markle, who would later be crucial to our efforts to close the rackets. In his campaign speeches, Jahn explained to the voters that the court over which he hoped to preside frequently handled family law matters such as divorce, adoptions, juvenile matters, and child custody hearings. Because of these responsibilities, Jahn argued that the job should be held by a married man. Donnie Markle, who had contracted polio as a youth and walked with the aid of crutches, was unmarried.

Judge Markle listened to Jahn's political speeches a few times without offering a rebuttal to this argument. Finally, at a campaign rally in Alta Loma, Markle decided to respond. "Folks," he said, "my opponent says that the work of the court makes it important that the presiding judge be a married man. If that's the case, then my opponent is eminently qualified, because he has been married five times!" The voters seemed to have appreciated this point, because Donnie Markle won the election.

By the time I was obtaining civil injunctions against illegal operations in Galveston, Eddie Jahn was married to a woman who was the proprietress of a bordello in Galveston. Eddie continued to hold public office as the city recorder, while practicing law on the side. One can imagine Mr. and Mrs. Jahn comparing notes at the end of the day—he sharing news from municipal court and she recounting her day at the bordello.

As the injunctions were issued by the court, the newspaper ran the names of the individuals and businesses cited for illegal activity. Eddie called me on the phone one day. "Jimmy," he said to me, "you know my wife runs a whorehouse. And I know you'll get around to filing an injunction against her sooner or later. Could you keep my name off the lawsuit? As a public official, I'd rather not read about myself in the newspaper."

"Eddie," I replied, "you know I can't do that under the rules of civil procedure. The law requires that I can't sue a married woman without including her husband in the same legal action. Under the rules of community property, you own half the whorehouse."

"Oh, I guess you're right," Eddie said. "I was just hoping you could do me a favor and keep me out of the paper."

Soon enough Eddie Jahn would have the sole responsibility for supporting the family, because Madame Jahn would be forced to go into retirement.

Meanwhile, at about the same time that we were obtaining injunctions against the gamblers, a runaway grand jury was conducting an investigation of the rackets. It issued a report on September 28, 1957, stating, "The conditions found ... to have existed in this county and (with) the apparent consent to such conditions by local officials is wholly inconsistent with honest government and with the oath of office taken by elected officials."

The grand jury also reported that its investigation showed that the "prostitution, gambling, and illicit liquor traffic form a breeding ground for the narcotics racket.... Where apathy toward law enforcement exists and where such apathy creates the unwholesome conditions which we know to exist, such conditions are bound to have an adverse effect upon each segment of our county and upon each of us individually.... The fact cannot be ignored that a sound economy can never be made to rest on such an unstable foundation, which undermines home life, corrupts our youth, and hampers the witness of the church.... Eternal vigilance is the price of liberty." The grand jury also pointed out that the many operators of the illegal businesses had criminal records, "which included such offenses as armed robbery, burglary, murder, and narcotics violations."

The unanimous report showed that there were indeed citizens who opposed gambling and corruption. Perhaps Jefferson's concept of a government of the people and by the people was not really dead after all.

So voluminous were our records and the documents that we actually had to open a separate office of the Texas Attorney General a few blocks away from the courthouse and in the center of the gambling empire. The vast majority of the credit for this success should go to Attorney General Will Wilson and the two citizen investigators—Buddy Givens and Carroll Yaws— who had proven themselves to be courageous and honest.

People have asked, was it all worth it?

Galveston and the Rackets 137

After the crackdown, I was sitting in my office on Galveston Island when I received a telephone call from a local housewife.

"Mr. Simpson, I am the mother of four children, and it is no easy task to provide the necessities of life for them. In the past, my husband's wages found their way into the craps tables, slot machines, and other illegal enterprises. Now I have a fair shot at using that money to put shoes on little feet, a roof over our head, and a better life for our family. Thank you so much."

Was it all worth it? You bet your boots it was.

Jim as Texas City Man of the Year in 1958.

138   Flak Bait

Jim's parents, Eva and Polk Simpson, at their 50th wedding anniversary.

The Simpson men: from the left, Bob, Dick, father Polk, Joe, and Jim about 1958.

Galveston and the Rackets **139**

Family photo for Jim's 1960 race for Congress. From the left, Jamie, Jim, Scott, Connie, and Simone.

SEND
JIM SIMPSON
TO CONGRESS

•

LEADERSHIP
FOR THE
NINTH CONGRESSIONAL DISTRICT

•

VOTE FOR A DEMOCRAT
IN THE DEMOCRATIC PARTY

Campaign poster, 1960.

SEND

JIM SIMPSON

TO

CONGRESS

LEADERSHIP FOR THE NINTH CONGRESSIONAL DISTRICT

Vote for a Democrat in the Democratic Primary

WHO IS JIM SIMPSON?

- Practicing attorney in Texas City for ten years.
- Native Texan—38 years old.
- Combat Veteran of World War II—59 missions over Europe—Air Medal with 2 silver clusters.
- Graduate University of Texas Law School.
- Former FBI agent principally engaged in investigating Communist subversion.
- Leader in suppression of organized crime.
- Texas City's Outstanding Young Man of the Year Award in 1958.
- Active Democrat.
- Married and 3 children.
- Member: Memorial Lutheran Church; VFW; American Legion; Kiwanis Club; President, Mainland Legal Society.

U. S. AIR FORCE
WORLD WAR 2

Campaign brochure, 1960. Jim lost to Clark Thompson, son-in-law of Col. W. L. Moody.

Galveston and the Rackets **141**

TEXAS CITY'S OUTSTANDING
YOUNG MAN IN 1948

SEE AND HEAR SIMPSON ON TV

•

KHOU-TV — Channel 11, Houston
Friday, April 27 - - 10:15 - 10:30 P.M.
Thursday, May 3 - 9:30 - 10:00 P.M.
Friday, May 4 - - - - 5:25 - 5:30 P.M.

•

KZTU-TV—Channel 10, Corpus Christi
Friday, May 4 - - - - 8:30 - 9:00 P.M.

kind—poverty, ignorance, tyranny, disease and war.

I will serve no group, but instead will be devoted to ideals, goals and hopes for our country. The cause of America is the cause of all mankind and of freedom-loving peoples everywhere.

I ask your help, your vote, your hand, your counsel, and your guidance. Together we shall win, not for Jim Simpson, but for the Ninth Congressional District, for our country, and for these goals to which I am deeply committed.

JIM, JIMMY, SCOTT,
CONNIE AND SIMONE SIMPSON

Brochure pages from Jim's unsuccessful race for Congress in 1960.

**Fifty Years of
Law Practice**

Jim outside his Texas City law office in about 1960.

Defending Motherhood and the Right to a Public Education

After the rackets were closed, I resigned my position as special assistant attorney general and returned to my law practice. As a husband and father, I had substantial responsibilities and—most of the time—inadequate resources with which to meet those obligations. I had diverted a great deal of my time to public service, and now I was determined to seriously pursue my law practice in order to provide for my family.

While I was eager to earn a good living, I also felt a duty to assist those in need without regard to their ability to pay. Foremost among these cases was one in which I represented a young woman who was a student at Alvin High School in Brazoria County. The case was recorded as *Kathy Cooper vs. Alvin Independent School District*.

Kathy Cooper was a high school senior at Alvin High School when she became pregnant. She had no thought of abortion, but instead she concentrated on supporting herself and her baby. She married the father with a dismal result. Many people feel a marriage is made in heaven. Apparently, this one was made in Madison Square Garden. Her husband was an uncaring and irresponsible fellow who did little to ease her path in life. Ultimately, the marriage became intolerable, and she obtained a divorce.

Kathy Cooper later applied for readmission to her high school in order to complete her education. The Alvin School District informed her they had a rule against unwed mothers attending public school. She sought to reason with the school officials, pointing out that she would need as much education as possible in order to support her child. Her plea fell on deaf ears, and her appeal to a board of trustees was rejected.

Her appeal was heard by a board of seven members.

Fortunately, one of them was a lawyer, O. G. Wellborn, who cast the sole vote in favor of her readmission. While the student had no money to pay, Wellborn nonetheless brought suit to force her readmission. I'm sure this did not increase his popularity on the school board. The legal counsel for the school district promptly moved to disqualify Wellborn on the grounds that, as a school board trustee, he was a party to the lawsuit, which therefore posed a conflict of interest.

Wellborn happened to be a law partner of my old law school classmate and friend, Charles W. Britt. The two of them knew they needed to find a new lawyer, and so Britt asked me to take over as Kathy Cooper's counsel. I was struck by the incredible injustice of the matter and agreed to take her case.

Soon I was standing before Judge G. P. Hardy, seeking an injunction to forbid the school district from denying Kathy Cooper a public education. At a hearing in Angleton a lawyer of my acquaintance stopped by the courtroom to speak to me and inquired whether I thought Judge Hardy would reinstate her as a student. I told him I didn't know if Judge Hardy would, but I verily believed Judge Warren would. Earl Warren was then Chief Justice of the U.S. Supreme Court.

Without much delay, Judge Hardy issued an injunction requiring Kathy Cooper to be readmitted to Alvin High School.

I could not believe that in the mid 1960s it could be seriously advocated that motherhood was a proper basis for the denial of a public education. Since the days of the Republic, Texas had long supported the concept and the value of a free public education. We knew that the community supported the banning of mothers in the school—even mothers such as Kathy Cooper, whose baby was born within marriage. So it was not surprising that the school district immediately filed an appeal.

The school district was represented by one of the finest school lawyers in the state, Joe Reynolds. Reynolds met with the board of trustees, who reaffirmed their intention of blocking the schoolhouse door against Kathy Cooper.

The next step in the process was for the attorneys on both sides to present an argument before the Court of Civil Appeals in Houston. After the passage of some time, the case was set for oral argument before the Houston appellate court, presided over by Chief Justice Spurgeon Bell. Justice Bell came from a background similar to my own. We had both grown up in Coryell County and had graduated from the University of Texas School of Law. He was a courtly gentleman and known for being fair. His philosophy however differed from my own.

On oral argument I sought to capture the attention of the appellate judges. My opening remarks went along these lines: "May it please your Honors. For the first time in the history of our Republic it has been asserted that motherhood is a sufficient basis for the denial of a free public education." The chief justice inquired of me, "Counsel, is that what this case is really all about?"

I replied, "Your Honor, that is exactly what it is all about."

My adversary, Joe Reynolds, able lawyer that he is, made as fine an argument as could have been fashioned.

My experience suggested that we could expect an opinion from the Court of Appeals in the coming months. Meanwhile, I had thought of our next move in the event the Court of Appeals reversed the trial court.

Within a week of the oral arguments, Justice Bell handed down the unanimous opinion of the Court approving of the action of the trial court and its reinstatement of Kathy Cooper as a student of Alvin Independent School District.

Now came the wait to see if the Alvin school district would attempt to appeal the case to the Texas Supreme Court. I had only one other ace in the hole. In my arguments before the trial court I had asserted a constitutional issue, which might have persuaded the United States Supreme Court to agree to hear the case. Fortunately, my fears were not justified. The school district elected to quit spending the taxpayers' money fighting an 18-year-old girl who just wanted to continue her education to support her child.

I had thought that my actions in the case would have found support within the community. I was amazed to find that more people seemed to disagree with my position than support it.

Later, I was greatly pleased to learn that a reporting service listed *Kathy Cooper v. Alvin Independent School District* as one of the most significant cases of the year. It stands as good law today. While I was never paid for my efforts, it remains one of my most gratifying cases.

A Decade of Free Dry Cleaning

Much of my work as a lawyer was in the field of workers' compensation. In these cases I represented men and women who had sustained an injury in the course of their employment. It was not the most remunerative area of law practice, but it was a great opportunity to be of help to workers at a time when they needed it the most. This required a thorough understanding of the Texas Workers Compensation Act and considerable knowledge in the field of traumatic injuries.

When a lawyer obtains compensation for his injured client, it's my opinion that he needs to take the extra step of advising the client on how best to invest the proceeds of the settlement. Early in my career I learned that unless the average worker had a lawyer or someone trustworthy who could help with the investment of a monetary settlement, he faced many opportunities to squander his money. Too often I had witnessed a worker receive a considerable lump sum, perhaps $25,000, only to learn that he had foolishly invested all of it in some get-rich-quick scheme advised by a brother-in-law or someone else with limited judgment or knowledge.

One of the workers I represented was Everett McCann, who was injured on the job at Monsanto Chemical Co. When I obtained a fair settlement for him, he needed advice on how to invest his funds productively. Initially, he had no notion of what to do with the money. I determined that McCann had been a fair student in high school and was an intelligent person. So I suggested that he explore the opportunity to find an ongoing business that might be for sale. If he found such a business he agreed to call me, and we would meet with my accountant, who could examine the books of the company in question and determine if the financial records justified his investment. McCann identified a dry cleaning business that was for sale, and we consulted my accountant.

The accountant reported back to me and to McCann that the business appeared to be sound and potentially profitable. It was a small cleaning and laundry shop which had a relatively low overhead and had done well, even without a great deal of business acumen on the part of the owner.

When presented with all the facts, it appeared to McCann and to me that the dry cleaning business would be a good investment. It turned out that I had been a customer of the shop myself, and therefore I had some slight knowledge of the business and its owner. McCann bought the enterprise largely with funds from his settlement. I urged him to be conservative with his money, maintain a low overhead, and emphasize good customer service.

McCann operated the business himself, without any employees. He worked hard to deliver good service and run an efficient shop. Soon the business was yielding a fair profit margin.

I continued to patronize the shop, and the business grew. I had urged Mr. McCann to read a book I had read many years earlier, *How to Win Friends and Influence People*. McCann learned the lessons of the book and put them to good use.

He refused to bill me for my dry cleaning. I chided him about such a lapse in good business practices, but he wouldn't take my money. He operated the business profitably for ten years, during which he avoided going into debt. Then he sold the business for a good profit. I had warned him not to sell unless he found a good job to replace his income from the business.

He landed a good job at the Texas A&M University Galveston campus before selling out, and at this writing, remains well employed. The only person more pleased with his success than I am is Everett McCann himself. The fee I earned in handling his case did not enable me to take early retirement. But the case afforded me—in addition to a decade of free dry cleaning—a considerable measure of satisfaction.

High School and the First Amendment

I have always believed that First Amendment rights are sacred. I was therefore delighted to serve as counsel for a student named Richard Egner who had been expelled from Texas City High School. Egner's sin was publishing a small newspaper, referred to in those days as an "underground newspaper."

While I considered handling First Amendment cases to be my duty as a lawyer and a citizen, I'm glad I didn't have to depend on them to feed my family. Once again, I had the privilege of defending the Constitution free of charge.

At the time of his expulsion, young Egner ranked very close to the top of his class at Texas City High School. What a shame it would be to deny this idealistic and bright youngster the benefits of a public education. The school authorities thought otherwise and expelled him on the grounds that he did not have the school's permission to distribute a newspaper.

Egner's parents promptly came to my door seeking assistance for their son. The father, Robert Egner, was one of the foremost authorities in America on the famous philosopher Lord Bertrand Russell of England. Despite his academic credentials, the family could not afford to pour money into litigation. I was happy to represent the young publisher. My partner at the time, Don B. Morgan, assisted me with the case. Don went on to a distinguished career as state district judge of the 212th District Court in Galveston before retiring to Austin, where he continues to serve as a visiting judge.

A First Amendment case can command the attention of both state and federal courts. My belief was that state courts were just as good a venue for First Amendment cases as federal courts in Galveston County.

Procedure required that I bring suit for injunction against the school district, its superintendent, and its board of trustees, virtually all of whom were well known to me. One trustee was my dentist, and another was my veterinarian and long-time friend. They were all persons of good will, but the trustees seemed to me to take too lightly the command of the First Amendment establishing a free press. In one of its few editions the little school paper stated on the front page, "We seek to be a journal of free expression and we seek suggestions from students and members of the school district on the serious and important topics of our times." The newspaper aspired to cover challenging issues such as the war in Vietnam, the war on poverty, and federal aid to education.

The school district never alleged that the newspaper contained anything salacious, pornographic, or defamatory. The sole criticism of the school district was that the newspaper violated a rule that no publication could be distributed at the high school without the prior approval of the principal.

I was hard pressed to find anything improper about the fledging publication. The school's lawyer, Holman Lilienstern, was an old comrade of mine in World War II. He and I had served on the front lines in Germany in the 104th Infantry Division. I hasten to point out that Lilienstern was a lieutenant colonel in Intelligence while I was a technical sergeant on air liaison with his division.

Lilienstern, on behalf of the school district, sought to remove my case from state to federal court. Judge Hugh Gibson was assigned to hear the case in state court, but he had already signaled in open court that he was sympathetic to the Egner position. The federal judge promptly remanded the case back to the state court, saying that state judges are just as capable of enforcing First Amendment rights as are federal judges.

Finally, the case was called for final hearing on the merits.

Before hearing it in final form, Judge Gibson ordered both parties to appear once more before the school district board of trustees, giving them one last opportunity to comply with the First Amendment. It was a mere formality. Once again the board of trustees voted 7-0 to bar Richard Egner from school.

After the final appearance before the school board, Judge Gibson entered a permanent injunction forbidding the school taking further action to bar Egner from attending school. The right to a free press was preserved, even in the corridors of high school.

As the saga of *Egner vs. Texas City High School* came to a close, there may have been some hurt feelings on both sides among the lawyers. But these have since been forgotten, and Holman Lilienstern and I, old comrades from the German front, are still warm friends.

Banking at the Sailor's Retreat

When a worker is injured on the job at a major industry, the employee is limited in what he may receive in compensation according to the terms of the Texas Workers Compensation Act. If a person is injured through the negligence of a company other than his own employer, then the limitation does not apply. A lawyer fortunate enough to obtain cases of this nature knows at the outset that he has a fair chance of getting adequate compensation for his client.

Such a case came to my door in the form of three men, each of whom had sustained severe injuries while working for Monsanto Company. While they were cleaning out a ditch on the edge of the plant operated by Monsanto, their employer, a Monsanto subcontractor, failed to warn them of highly inflammable chemicals in the ditch. My clients were burned when one of them lit a cigarette.

The three, Jesus Limones, Bennie Delorosa, and one other man whose name I cannot now recall, appeared in my office and requested that I seek compensation for the injuries they had suffered. The suit was against Malone Trucking Company, which had been hired by Monsanto to pump out the explosive chemicals stored in the ditch adjacent to the chemical plant. I filed suit against Malone Trucking and proceeded to take sworn depositions. After months of testimony, the defendant wanted to sit down with the plaintiffs and their lawyer to discuss a settlement.

Unfortunately, the injured workmen were highly suspicious of others. I got along with them well, in part because I speak Spanish, albeit with some difficulty. However, they were skeptical of all lawyers, even including the one they had hired. For the longest time, the injured men wanted to make outrageously high demands, the kind that would make settlement prohibitive. Gradually, I was able to break down their suspicions. They must have had unfortunate experiences with previous lawyers. Finally, they agreed in principle to an acceptable range of compensation.

I then turned my attention to getting the defendant's insurance company to agree to a settlement. Meanwhile, I had to persuade the injured men that if we were to take the case to trial, there would be no guarantees of a recovery. After some negotiation, we had a settlement offer on the table of a total of $60,000. I urged the men to accept the offer, pointing out the considerable risk they would run in litigation. With some reluctance, all three men agreed to accept the offer.

In due course, I received the settlement agreement, as well as a check for the agreed amount. Each of the men would receive about $20,000 when the smoke all cleared away. I explained to them that I would have them endorse the insurance company check, which would be deposited into my trust account at the bank. From that account I would write a check to each man. There was still considerable haggling on the part of the men, and I, at one time, told them they might be better served to let me try the case to a jury. Then the men warmed to the $60,000.

As I discussed writing each man a check for his share, they promptly said no, they would not agree to this. I explained to them that if I shortchanged them, they could have me prosecuted for embezzlement, which would cost me my law license.

They replied that unless they got cash, there was no settlement. By now, it was closing time at the bank, but I phoned a bank officer and had him explain to them the safety of taking their money in the form of a cashier's check or a certified check.

No dice. They simply did not trust me, nor any other person or institution. I finally broke the deadlock by asking them to accompany me to the bank, where they could see the money counted in their presence and handed to them in cash.

Near my office, there was a sleazy beer joint with a very unsavory reputation called the Sailor's Retreat. Despite the enormous stack of greenbacks in their possession, they insisted on leaving the bank and calling their friends to help them celebrate their windfall.

How strange it was that they would not trust a bank officer, a bank, or reputable lawyers. Instead they placed all their trust in the Sailor's Retreat, where they intended to consume large amounts of beer. I wished Jesus, Bennie, and the third man well—and hoped that they didn't get knocked on the head and relieved of all of their newfound riches.

Starting College of the Mainland

The best way to take the measure of a person is to ask, "Who are your heroes?" One of my heroes for many years has been Mirabeau B. Lamar, who was one of Texas's earliest statesmen. Many consider him the father of the Texas public education system. An excellent university in Beaumont bears his name.

Lamar once observed, "An educated mind is the guardian

genius of democracy." My father was unemployed during much of the Depression years and was a man of very few resources. He desperately wanted each of his eight children to have a formal education beyond high school. The means to provide such education was set in motion by the bombing of Pearl Harbor and the beginning of World War II.

While I was away at the war in Europe, the G.I. Bill of Rights was being established back home in America. Its cornerstone, the education component, largely provided the financial wherewithal for a veteran to earn a bachelor's degree. Prior to the enactment of the G.I. Bill, my family had concluded I would serve as an apprentice to a welder as a means of learning a trade. So I owe a great debt to the G.I. Bill and public higher education. In light of this, I was eager to advance educational opportunity in my own community.

One of the pioneers in the effort to establish a community college in Galveston County was my dear friend and labor leader, Paul Teague. Teague was a big man by any measure. He bore the nickname "Tiny" because he was about seven feet tall and weighed about 300 pounds. Teague was a man of firm convictions and of impeccable honor. Even his adversaries in the labor relations world recognized that he was a man of his word—you could take it to the bank. Once he had given his word and his handshake, there was no turning back.

In spite of the fact that he had very little formal education, Teague had a deep commitment to the cause of education. In representing the interests of working men and women he knew well the impact education had on them and their families. He also understood how difficult it was for young people growing up in communities without major educational institutions.

In 1966, as a leader in Galveston County, Teague became involved in plans for establishing a community college in Texas City. This would enable the children of working class families to get at least two years of college level credit before leaving the county to continue their education. Committees were formed to study the feasibility of creating a county-wide community college district. Teague soon took a major role in forming the community college district with taxing authority to support the endeavor.

Teague called me one day to ask if I might be interested in serving on the board of the proposed college district. I knew that the cost of sending a young person to Austin, College Station, or Lubbock could be a heavy burden for many working families in our community.

My experience at the University of Texas from 1945 to 1950 had impressed upon me the value of education. I jumped at the chance to help launch the new community college. Soon I was sworn in as a member of the founding board of this new institution, College of the Mainland.

Of course, there were no bricks and mortar. We had no campus, and indeed, we had no structures of any kind. Board meetings were held in a spare office in a bank building in La Marque.

Johnny Henderson, one of the greatest advocates of the new college, was a leader in the African American community in Galveston County and was vice president of the Texas AFL-CIO. He grew up in poverty and segregation and knew first hand of the injustices in our land. He understood that education was the solution to many of our societal woes. He was an early supporter of the effort to found the college district, which would provide the tax revenue to build a campus.

Unfortunately, many citizens of the district opposed having a new taxing entity, and it became evident that a referendum to establish the college district would fail in the more conservative precincts. Johnny Henderson was the leader in gaining support within the African American community. Without that support, the measure would not have passed.

Johnny conceived the idea of escorting labor leader Paul Teague and me to every African American church in the district to spread the gospel about the importance of voting for the college district and its taxing authority. On the Sunday morning before the election, Johnny arranged that the three of us would speak in each and every church. After a generous introduction extolling the virtues of the speakers, we would all vie for who most frequently invoked the names of Martin Luther King Jr., John F. Kennedy, and Abraham Lincoln.

I had recently acquired a new navy blue Cadillac four-door sedan with all the bells and whistles. As I drove the three of us on our rounds, Teague sat in the front passenger seat and Henderson was ensconced in the back seat. Along our route, every street corner had a group of parishioners dressed in their Sunday finest on their way to church. At some point, Henderson observed, "I do declare, Simpson, the age of equality has done come at last. Here is my old black ass, seated in the back end of a new Cadillac, driven by a white lawyer as my chauffeur."

Our strategy proved to be a success, because the following Tuesday the voters went to the polls and cast the necessary votes to breathe life into the new college.

The first task facing the board was the crucial one of naming a president. There was little experience among the board members in choosing a college president. While we had no notion as to who should become the first president, we all seemed to have some criteria in mind. Foremost in my mind was the need for naming a president who had a firm understanding and commitment to the concept of academic freedom.

During my early days at UT, I observed the result of undue influence exerted by a board of regents upon the administration and faculty of a great university. At UT, conditions had been so oppressive that the regents had the nerve to demand the firing of an economics professor simply because they disagreed with some of his opinions in a public discourse.

Stifling academic freedom can destroy the very purpose of higher education. I did not want to see our fledgling institution challenged by governance that threatened free speech and intellectual freedom.

In addition to Teague, another real leader on the board was H. K. ("Griz") Eckert, who prior to retirement, had been a widely respected captain of industry. One of the first persons we interviewed while searching for a president was Herbert

Stallworth, who held a position of leadership at a college in Tennessee. He was a man of the Old South, but he devoutly believed in the cause of education, academic freedom, and equality under the law.

In an interview, my first question of Stallworth was whether or not the U.S. Supreme Court had correctly decided *Brown vs. State Board of Education*, the opinion that ultimately struck down the concept of segregation and "separate but equal" education. When Stallworth gave an eloquent argument in support of the court's decision in *Brown*, I knew who would receive my vote to be the first president of College of the Mainland.

Much more discussion ensued, but in the end, Herb Stallworth was named president. We could not have made a better choice. Stallworth, working with Teague, Eckert, and others, got the college off to a good start. Issues such as religious freedom and social equality would later arise, but the tenor and values set by the founding board and its president served as a strong foundation.

During these early years, the society at large was shaking off the shackles of segregation. An atmosphere of freedom and equality took root at our young college, which, in part, was a reflection of the values of its founders.

I was later to serve two terms as president of the board of trustees and one term as president of the Texas Association of Community College Trustees. I was a member of the board of the college for 23 years.

It had fallen my lot to fight in Europe in the Second World War, to serve as a special agent of the FBI, and to serve as Assistant Attorney General of Texas in the fight to destroy organized crime in Texas. But there is no other endeavor of which I am more proud than the role I played in the founding and nurturing of the college.

As Daniel Webster said to the U.S. Supreme Court in arguing the famous Dartmouth College case, "It is only a small college, your honors, but there are those of us who love it." I feel the same about College of the Mainland.

Death on the Highway

Most of my courtroom work as a trial lawyer over the course of 50 years was in the field of personal injury law. Most often, I represented the injured party, although on rare occasion, I was called on to represent a defendant. However, when asked to defend, I always confessed to the insurance carrier or the corporate executive in charge that my heart was not really with the defense. I had seen so much stress and consternation among the injury victims I had represented in five decades of law practice that it was hard to change gears and work for the other side.

In representing plaintiffs, I always felt entrusted with my clients' lives. It was a special burden that I gladly bore. In 1988 Deonna Acree, the 26-year-old wife of my client, Greg Acree, was driving the family car from their residence along Farm-to-Market Road 646 in Galveston County. She was on her way to a drugstore in the Clear Lake area, where she worked as a pharmacy clerk. During her commute, her vehicle was struck head on by an 18-wheeler traveling on the wrong side of the road.

Congress had passed a law containing many safety regulations designed to curb the carnage of high speed, essentially dangerous vehicles. A truck driver is required to limit his driving to a set number of hours each week to avoid fatigue. He is also required to have his truck inspected regularly to ensure that it is safely maintained. We discovered that the driver of the 18-wheeler was guilty of many violations. The driver's log book contained evidence that the driver was suffering from fatigue. In fact, the log would later prove that the driver suffered fatigue that was comparable to driving while intoxicated.

As Mrs. Acree traveled along FM 646, the massive truck operated by Maersk Container Service Company, which was speeding, veered into the lane of oncoming traffic. It collided with the 26-year-old woman. Experts testified that a driver in her position would have had no more than three-quarters of a second to react.

The resulting head-on collision was of such force and violence as to destroy the small car, killing Deonna Acree almost instantly. I have often reflected that if her husband that morning had delayed his wife by asking her a single question, the tragedy would have been averted.

Her husband had a premonition that she was in danger. He sensed that something unusual had occurred as he got into his car and retraced her steps. Five minutes away from their residence he could see the flashing lights of the state highway patrol car ahead, and he knew in a flash that his wife was dead.

My heart went out to this young family and I was determined to do what I could to make sure her husband was adequately compensated and to do what I could to protect others from the same hazard.

My job was to demonstrate the negligence of the shipping company and the great loss suffered by the family. Maersk was an enormous international shipping company, so it would be well represented by the best defense attorneys. I tracked down and interviewed the few eyewitnesses to the accident.

I found an expert analyst in Phoenix who helped me review the Federal Motor Carrier Regulations and the violations that contributed to the accident. The driver in this case was not only suffering from extreme fatigue, but he also had a bad driving record and probably should not have been hired by Maersk in the first place. Plaintiffs' lawyers often serve the role of putting teeth in laws that are frequently ignored by industry. In many cases, regulation is lax and fines are too insignificant to change illegal behavior. But large jury awards get the attention of corporate executives and shareholders. Litigation such as this serves to enforce the law by making violations more visible to the public and providing an incentive for companies to behave responsibly.

I secured a setting for the trial of the case in District Court in Galveston, and as the day of trial loomed the insurance carrier finally began to take the case seriously.

In those days I was assisted by Timothy A. Beeton, a talented trial lawyer who was then my partner, along with my other able partner, my daughter Simone. Not long after, we were joined by my son Greg. So the firm was composed of three Simpsons, Tim, and our longtime associate Laurette Williams. It was a great team. Today, Tim's Galveston law practice still bears the name of our old firm, Simpson and Beeton.

Finally on the day before the trial was scheduled to begin, the insurance carrier offered the family $2.4 million. This was a record settlement for a case of this type in Galveston County at the time. Moreover, it forced the trucking company to take responsibility for the unsafe practices of its drivers, thereby making the roads safer for us all.

Madalyn Murray O'Hair

In the early days after the founding of College of the Mainland, there appeared to be a consensus of agreement among the trustees regarding fundamental issues such as academic freedom and free speech. We had agreed that the U.S. Constitution would be our guide when we were faced with controversy.

I observed at one meeting that our objective should be to establish the college as a place where free discussion on any topic would be encouraged. I wanted this freedom to nurture the exchange of ideas. When I said this, Herb Stallworth, the first president of the college, immediately amended my goal to embrace a *civilized* clash of ideas. He is the most gentle, civilized man I have ever met.

We all knew the voters in the college district were conservative. I always sought to offer my counsel to President Stallworth without attempting to press my own ideas. Dr. Stallworth seemed to be a good advocate for the concepts the board sought to implement. Early in Dr. Stallworth's administration, I sensed danger when I read in the local newspapers of a developing furor over an invitation extended to atheist Madalyn Murray

O'Hair to speak at the college. In a speaker series entitled, "Great Issues," the college invited prominent Americans to address the issues of the day. Among the speakers were Senator Barry Goldwater, broadcast journalist Roger Mudd, and others of all walks of life and shades of opinion. Nevertheless, I knew immediately upon reading of the O'Hair invitation that this was not the average controversial speaker. Sure enough, the ink had hardly dried on the newspaper report before a hue and cry arose over her prospective appearance. One gentleman from League City, in a bombastic tone, swore he would never again vote for me as a trustee unless I voted to rescind the O'Hair invitation. Another was so irate that he threatened the destruction of my law practice and other misfortune. I tried to mollify him with words such as, "every American has a right to his or her own ideas." But he remained adamant that O'Hair should not be permitted on campus. He then proceeded to threaten me with serious bodily injury unless I changed my views. Conscience compelled me to tell him that where the Constitution was concerned I was not willing to make compromises.

Several board members expressed the view that we should listen to outraged citizens and rescind the invitation. One Baptist minister, at a public meeting of the trustees, inquired of President Stallworth, "Are you a Christian?" I ended that line of questioning by informing the minister that Dr. Stallworth's religious beliefs were no one's business but his own.

The issue rocked back and forth for a number of weeks, during which the board took no action to rescind O'Hair's invitation.

While I could not agree with many parts of her agenda, I could not and did not bring myself to knuckle under to the demands of far right wing bigotry. I later learned that many people who came to hear O'Hair concluded that she made a constructive and stimulating talk. College of the Mainland had weathered its first, if not last, assault on the First Amendment.

I might observe, however, that standing up for ideas slightly out of the mainstream comes with a price. After this episode I had to be more and more cautious about accepting as jurors in my civil cases those who harbored bitter opinions about the importance of unlimited and free debate.

A Tranquil and Steady Dedication

As I look back on my life and the crucial influences and turning points that shaped my journey, I know I benefited from my mother's strong will and commitment to her family. I was blessed to learn the value of hard work from my rural, and at times, impoverished, upbringing. There is no doubt in my mind that the Second World War exposed me to life-transforming experiences and opportunities. The University of Texas opened many doors that enriched my intellectual life and trained me for a career in law.

My optimism and my respect for honest government compelled me to fight gambling, prostitution, and other vice when I encountered it. But I became friends with many of the men I arrested in the years that followed the crackdown, and I remain so today. I am concerned that there are those who favor a return to gambling as a form of economic development for Galveston County. I oppose it for the same reasons I did so long ago.

More often than not, as a lawyer, I have represented the underdog. I suppose living through the Depression gave me an affinity for the laborer rather than the corporation. I have fought more battles for the injured, the maimed, and the afflicted, not to mention the widows and children of men and women lost to industrial and highway accidents.

I learned a great respect for the Constitution, even if it meant having to sue my friends, neighbors, and local elected officials to enforce our Constitutional protections in our schools and government. We must be vigilant, and in my experience, you have only to look around to find examples of encroachment upon our Constitutional rights. If we sit idly by and watch these rights be undermined, even by people with good intentions, we will wake up and discover that we have lost Jefferson's dream.

In an adversarial profession, I have tried to treat my colleagues and opponents with respect. Indeed, many of my worthy opponents have joined the ranks of my friends after we settled our differences at the courthouse. The same has been true of the old racketeers I once placed in jail. A few years ago I stopped by a local coffee shop, where unbeknownst to me, some of the old gamblers congregated every morning for breakfast and conversation. I encountered Pete Salvato, Carlo Emmite, and several others, men whose businesses I had closed and perhaps some of whom I had placed in jail almost 50 years earlier. But after all this time, Pete and the others greeted me warmly, like old adversaries who had earned each other's respect, and invited me to join them. I rejoiced in the fact that they were not bitter toward me.

I admire Adlai Stevenson's view of patriotism, expressed in a speech to the American Legion in 1952: "I venture to suggest that what we mean is a sense of national responsibility which will enable America to remain master of her power—to walk with it in serenity and wisdom, with self-respect and the respect of all mankind; a patriotism that puts country ahead of self; a patriotism which is not short, frenzied outbursts of emotion, but the tranquil and steady dedication of a lifetime. These are words that are easy to utter, but this is a mighty assignment. For it is often easier to fight for principles than to live up to them."

I certainly have my share of human imperfection, and I am sure that I earned some of the flak I've encountered along the way. But I hope that my eight decades of living have demonstrated some of the characteristics Stevenson espoused. That over the years I have both fought for principles—and lived up to them—with the tranquil and steady dedication of a lifetime.

Fifty Years of Law Practice **165**

The brood in Dickinson—Greg, Jamie, Scott, Simone, and Jim.

Family portrait at home on Dickinson Bayou about 1973. Scott, Jim, Greg, Simone, Jamie, and Connie.

Seven Simpson siblings: from left, Dick, Marvel, Joe, Lynn, Bob, Jim, and Pat at Joe's ranch in Cypress Mill, Texas.

Connie and Jim dancing at Simone's wedding, 1978.

168   Flak Bait

Fiftieth anniversary portrait, December 2002

Jim in about 2000.

Appendix

The one great rule of composition is to speak the truth.
—Thoreau

The Texas Observer

We will serve no group or party but will hew hard to the truth as we find it and the right as we see it.

An Independent Liberal Weekly Newspaper

Vol. 49   JUNE 14, 1957   10c per copy   No. 5

Three Men Who Cracked an Empire

Place a Bet-- Take a Note

TEXAS CITY

"You feel like you are a hell of a long way from home."

That is the tense, nervous reaction Carroll S. Yaws, 37, Alta Loma, and Jimmy Givens, 33, LaMarque, felt as they repeatedly went unarmed into the Maceo gambling syndicate's plush Balinese Room casino gathering evidence for Atty. Gen. Will Wilson.

Yaws recalls: "You go through

Bob Bray

six doors from one street to the gambling room as you walk 75 yards out over the water. It would be a long way to have to come back in a hurry."

Givens, Galveston County Democratic chairman and president of the Galveston County Young Democrats, said that his closest call of the eleven-weeks investigation was not at the Balinese Room but at an establishment known as the Ranch House near Kemah. An employee of the place was within two feet of a notebook which would have given them away.

Carroll Yaws, Jim Simpson, and Jim (Buddy) Givens
Two Oilworkers and an ex-FBI Agent Who Worked Together to Break Up the Games

Givens and Yaws, both married men, were selected by Special Asst. Atty. Gen. Jim Simpson of Texas City to take the lead in the exceedingly touchy task of gathering evidence against Galveston County's illegal operations.

Simpson, who backed only eight votes winning the county attorney's office while campaigning for cleaning up gambling, knew that both men were opposed to "open county" operations. "I knew they were deeply dedicated to ridding the county of organized crime, and I felt they had the intelligence and judgement to do the job," he said. "But I was not sure they would do it. Not many men will agree to accept such a responsibility and take the physical risk and abuse that goes with such an investigation. I talked to them individually, not even telling them who his partner would be, and after careful consideration, both accepted the task."

After a careful briefing from former FBI agent Simpson, the two citizen investigators, both of whom are regular employees of oil companies on the mainland and members and former officers of the Oil, Chemical, and Atomic Workers International Union Local 499, started infiltrating gambling joints, saloons, and bawdy houses. They worked two weeks in the smaller places before moving in on the more cautiously operated Maceo syndicate establishments.

"We wanted to get a bit of experience, learn how to act and how to get information, before we started after the B-Room," explained Givens.

In the course of the investigation they spent more than $3,000 furnished by Atty. Gen. Wilson, secured hundreds of pages of information on illegal operations, and poured out dozens of glasses of whisky. They would map each night's program of visits, hitting all the places in a given geographical area. On their busiest night they visited 17 establishments. Sometimes they would be in a place only a couple of minutes, other times for a couple of hours.

(Continued on page 5)

DEATH-THROES OF A WIDE-OPEN ERA

Wilson Slams Dice, Bawds

GALVESTON COUNTY

For more than 20 years, Rev. Harry Burch, a slender, scholarly, soft-spoken man, has been a leader in the fight against gambling and other illegal operations in Galveston County.

He and members of his Paul's Union Church in LaMarque forced gambling czar Sam Maceo to pull his slot machines out of their community. They have been participants in every crusade that has sprung up since; and there have been several.

Last Sunday Rev. Burch paused in his sermon for an announcement which made him "very happy."

"Never," he said, "during the long fight to rid the county of organized crime, have I told you the victory was in sight. I now have reason to believe that we are 'round the corner.' Next day even the skeptic had to agree that he might well be right.

Atty. Gen. Will Wilson, in a decisive blow which Galveston County will never forget, proved once and for all that when he said he would close down Galveston it was not "campaign ballyhoo." When his ten assistant attorneys general, headed by Cecil Rotsch, head of the law enforcement division, and James P. Simpson, appointed specially to help out with the Galveston cleanup, filed nearly 50 injunction suits, it was too late for the gamblers even to sneak a look at their hole cards. The game was over.

Word spread like wildfire from the courthouse and along Market Street that the suits were being filed, and even as Rotsch and his men were still working with the petitions, dozens of groups of men congregated to talk of the crackdown in hushed, funereal tones.

The largest group of gamblers and others involved in similar activities gathered in front of the Turf Grill, the famed Maceo syndicate headquarters. Inside Joe Maceo and other officials of the organization scurried about.

As reporters walked along the street they were beset by politicians (Police Commissioner Walker Rourke, County Commissioner Jimmy Vacek, and others) and club owners wanting to know "which places" were named in the suits. Islanders were plainly shocked and a little frightened by a series of lawsuits which one man complained will "knock out businesses worth several million dollars."

Up on the second floor of Galveston County's ancient courthouse, District Clerk H. H. Tremont surveyed the scene with awe. "I've been in this office nearly 20 years and I've never seen this much activity before." As he talked his four clerks had formed a sort of assembly-line operation for fast processing of the petitions.

(Continued on Page 4)

The Rev. Harry Burch in his Study
Sam Maceo Came With Gifts, and He Left With Them
Photos by Bob Bray

Attorney General Will Wilson
He Did Exactly What He Said He'd Do

The front page of The Texas Observer, June 14, 1957.

Three Men Who Cracked an Empire

By Bob Bray
The Texas Observer
June 14, 1957

TEXAS CITY—"You feel like you are a hell of a long way from home."

That is the tense, nervous reaction Carroll S. Yaws, 37, Alta Loma, and Jimmy Givins, 33, La Marque, felt as they repeatedly went unarmed into the Maceo gambling syndicate's plush Balinese Room casino gathering evidence for Attorney General Will Wilson.

Yaws recalls: "You go through six doors from one street to the gambling room as you walk 75 yards out over the water. It would be a long way to have to come back in a hurry."

Givens, Galveston County Democratic chairman and president of the Galveston County Young Democrats, said that his closest call of the eleven-week investigation was not at the Balinese Room but at an establishment known as the Ranch House near Kemah. An employee of the place was within two feet of a notebook which would have given them away.

Givens and Yaws, both married men, were selected by Special Assistant Attorney General Jim Simpson of Texas City to take the lead in the exceedingly touchy task of gathering evidence against Galveston County's illegal operations.

Simpson, who lacked only eight votes winning the county attorney's office while campaigning for cleaning up gambling, knew that both men were opposed to "open county" operations. "I knew they were deeply dedicated to ridding the county of organized crime, and I felt they had the intelligence and judgment to do the job," he said. "But I was not sure they would do it. Not many men would agree to accept such a responsibility and take the physical risk and abuse that goes with such an investigation. I talked to them individually, not even telling them who his partner would be, and after careful consideration, both accepted the task.

"After a careful briefing from former FBI agent Simpson, the two citizen investigators, both of whom are regular employees of oil companies on the mainland and members and former officers of the Oil, Chemical, and Atomic Workers International Union Local 499, started infiltrating gambling joints, saloons, and bawdy houses. They worked two weeks in the smaller places before moving in on the more cautiously operated Maceo syndicate establishments.

"We wanted to get a bit of experience, learn how to act and how to get information, before we started after the B-Room," explained Givens.

In the course of the investigation they spent more than $3,000 furnished by Attorney General Wilson, secured hundreds of pages of information on illegal operations, and poured out dozens of glasses of whisky. They would map each night's program of visits, hitting all the places in a given geographical area. On their busiest night they visited 17 establishments. Sometimes they would be in a place only a couple of minutes, other times for a couple of hours.

Their work day started around 8 P.M. and would usually run until 2 A.M., sometimes much later. "They put in more than 30 such nights and yet carried their regular work loads at their company jobs. It was a tremendous physical effort aside from the nervous strain," Simpson declared.

The primary target, Simpson said, was the Maceo operations, which are the "principal syndicate" both on the island and the mainland.

Givens and Yaws visited the Turf Grill and Western Room headquarters of the syndicate within two weeks after they started their work. "The Western Room was the key to the Balinese Room," said Yaws. "We became acquainted with the receptionist there and one night after gambling at the Western Room we told her that we and our wives would like to go out to the Balinese Room for dinner. It was," Givins grinned, "Yaws's birthday and me and my wife's wedding anniversary. That was the truth. It really was."

The receptionist phoned the Balinese Room and made reservations for them, and they were in the heart of the Maceo gambling empire. "The service was excellent and the food was fine," Yaws said. He also noted that the gambling room had five dice tables, four of which were operating, three roulette tables, two blackjack tables, half a dozen slot machines and room for 150 players. They tried them all, conservatively; and on that score Yaws had a complaint.

"I put five dollars in a quarter slot machine before I finally won two quarters," he said. "That's a pretty rough return on your money, or I should say the state's money." He had put $5 in the machine because he had instructions to play it until it paid off so he could complete slot machine evidence. The meals and gambling for the two couples ran $62.

The investigators soon learned that a good way to get into the joints was to flash money. They carried clips with $100 or $50 bills on the outside of the roll and would sometimes pay for drinks with large bills. This frequently prompted the bartender to inquire if they "didn't want to try a hot craps game tonight?"

The system got them into plenty of gambling halls, but it almost led to their identity being discovered. They had flashed a big bill in a club at Kemah, and the bartender invited them to a "big game." They quickly accepted. The bartender climbed in his car, told them to follow, and roared off with tires screeching.

Givens recalled: "We had to keep up so we started up and followed. They only hitch was we had our leather notebooks with all information on our investigations in the glove compartment of the car. It was unlocked and we couldn't lock it because the key was in the ignition switch. When we arrived at the gambling house a Negro attendant and guard approached the car, told us to walk on in and they would park our car. We had to leave the notes unlocked in the car glove compartment," recalled Givens.

Yaws said, "You can be sure we made our bets there in a hurry and left as quick as we could. I just knew that attendant was going to take a peek in that glove compartment just to see what he could find. My old heart boomed every time the telephone rang or someone came in the door. But nothing happened and we got out without question."

Aside from the grueling hours of night life and day work, both investigators said the worst part was embarrassing incidents growing out of their frequenting the places. Both had been known by close friends as staunch opponents of gambling and vice operations. For them to start frequenting such places overnight was bound to cause talk.

One time Givens, attending a political meeting, was seated next to a minister who was a very close friend. "About halfway through the session I discovered that I had been lighting one cigarette after another with a book of matches I'd picked up at the Balinese Room," he said. "I'm sure he thought it quite strange."

—Reprinted with permission of
The Texas Observer.

Campaign Speech

James P. Simpson
Candidate for County Attorney, Galveston County
Democratic Primary
July 25, 1954

Good afternoon my fellow citizens of Galveston County. This is Jim Simpson coming before you today and asking you to exercise in his behalf one of your most precious rights—your vote—and to entrust him with the duty of being your county attorney. I realize that at this time of day my audience is composed largely of ladies, mothers, and housewives. And of that I am very glad because the things of which I wish to speak today are those matters in which I am sure the wives and mothers of our county are deeply interested. I have always insisted that we should have greater participation in government and politics on the part of women. And this is not with me merely a matter of equality. It is my firm belief that women are by their very nature more deeply concerned with the unwholesome conditions in any given area and that because of their status as wives and mothers they are more vitally interested in seeing a good environment in which to rear their children.

Before I go into the matter of law enforcement and other important matters, I would like to state a few facts concerning my background. During World War II, I served in Europe, flying 59 combat missions and participating in three major battles for which I was awarded the Air Medal and three battle stars. Following my discharge from military service, I enrolled at the University of Texas and upon graduation from the law school, I commenced practicing law in LaMarque in 1950. Shortly after commencing practice, I accepted an appointment as special agent of the FBI. Before going to duty as an FBI agent, I attended the FBI Academy up at the Marine Base at Quantico, Virginia. There I received the very finest instruction in criminal investigation, preparation of criminal cases, gathering of evidence, fingerprinting, scientific investigation and countless other subjects so essential to law enforcement. I then served for two years as an FBI agent throughout a large part of our country, and during that time I gained invaluable experience which I am sure will prove most helpful when I become your county attorney. During my service in the FBI I met a young lady who was also employed by the Bureau and we were married and we now have one baby girl. We live in Dickinson where I am engaged in the practice of civil and criminal law.

As a lawyer I have defended both capital and non-capital cases in several of which the extreme penalty of the law was asked by the State. Most of my experience has come in cases in which I was appointed by the district judges. I have also practiced in the appellate courts. I recently won a unanimous decision in the Court of Civil Appeals in which case I am presently appearing before the Supreme Court and I also have pending a case before the Court of Civil Appeals. So you can see I have had a wide and varied experience in criminal investigation, presentation of evidence, the defense of capital cases, and experience in appellate courts, all of which I believe well qualifies me for the office of county attorney.

Now there are five men in the race for county attorney, and it would seem fair for you to ask why does this fellow Jim Simpson want to be county attorney? Well, the answer is very simple. When I went to law school and when I served as an FBI agent and when I fought for this country during World War II the idea became very deeply ingrained in me that our government should be respected and that its laws should be obeyed. I have never been able to reconcile the existence of organized crime in our county and I never will. And so that in short is why I want to be your county attorney, because I am the only man in this race for county attorney who pledges to you that he will use every ounce of power placed in the statute books to end organized crime in the form of gambling, prostitution, the illegal sale of liquor, the sale of narcotics, and the sale of beer to minors. If Jim Simpson becomes your county attorney the toleration of criminals in our midst will cease to exist.

Now, why does Jim Simpson so deeply resent the existence of organized crime in our county, and why should you as wives and mothers be concerned with this problem? I think there are several reasons. First, we know that the heavy flow of narcotics, which finds its way into the hands of children, exists because we have in our county a large number of illegally operated places where criminals of the worst sort from all over the country abound. If you have ever seen, as I did while working as an FBI agent, a 15-year-old boy whose arm looked like a sieve from having injections of dope, then I know you would resent as much as I do these gamblers and other gangsters in our midst who provide the vehicle for the flow of narcotics. Secondly, we know that the existence of flagrant law violations is a major cause of juvenile delinquency. It is as simple as this. We cannot expect higher standards of conduct from our children than we ourselves set. Working as an FBI agent I saw at first hand the high rate of crime among children when children lived in an area where a wholesome respect for the law did not exist. Third, corruption in government. You simply do not have organized violations of the law existing alongside honest and dependable public officials. This fact has been made clear not only in our own county but throughout our state and our nation. This corruption in government causes our people to lose faith in the system under which we live and when we have lost faith in the system we have lost all that is worth fighting for. This matter of corrupting our government is something of deep concern to me. During World War II I, like millions of other Americans, risked my life for this government and I certainly do not like seeing the government for which I fought corrupted by a bunch of gangsters in our midst. Fourth, wherever conditions of gambling and other vices abound you always find crimes of violence flowing out of these conditions. Recently in Galveston, a reputable citizen came near to losing his life when a gunfight broke out in a gambling joint across the street from his office. This occurred on a Sunday morning at about 9:00 A.M. when you were probably getting ready to go to church. Now, do you think that we need in our county such people as this? Recently near Texas City, one gambler shot and seriously wounded another at 1:30 in the morning. The same thing occurs throughout the county very frequently.

Now there are those who would try to convince you that gambling and prostitution and other vices are an essential part of our economy. I think you know better than that. It is all too obvious that the only people who benefit from organized crime are those very, very few who refuse to work for a living but who instead prosper while violating our laws and corrupting our government, undermining the development of our youth and degrading everything that worthwhile citizens hold to be dear. To say that crime is economically sound is absurd when money that should flow through legitimate businesses for the purchase of worthwhile goods for family living is instead diverted to the unlawful element. It is certainly not economically sound. Without organized crime Galveston County would prosper much greater than it does today.

Now it may seem funny that one who seeks a position of law enforcement would announce simply that he intends to enforce the law. And yet it is a unique position, for Jim Simpson is the only candidate for county attorney who has absolutely pledged to enforce all the laws and to end organized crime. When Jim Simpson is elected your county attorney a wholesome respect for the law will commence and the wholesale violations of the law by certain groups and individuals will cease to exist. But Jim Simpson needs your help. I know that the good and decent and honest and law abiding citizens of our county are by far in the majority. I know we have the finest citizens of all the world and I say this advisedly because I have visited a large part of the world in the military service and I have traveled throughout most of our country while I served as an FBI agent. But it is going to require the effort of all worthwhile citizens to elect people to public office who believe in the majesty of the law and who are pledged to living up to the sacred oath which they take.

Now I feel have made my position clear to you, and to sum it up, it is simply this: When Jim Simpson becomes your county attorney he will exert every effort and he will use every law and every ounce of power provided him to end organized crime in our county. Jim Simpson is able to do just this because his past experience as an FBI agent, his experience as a defense attorney, and the courage exhibited in combat will qualify him to be your county attorney. Very soon now you will go to the polls to choose your next county attorney. Jim Simpson earnestly requests your vote and your support. The road we travel may be long and hard, but at the end lies a greater, a cleaner, and a more prosperous Galveston County. Your vote and support for Jim Simpson on July 25 will be deeply appreciated.

Padlock on the Balinese

Excerpts from
The Houston Press
June 10 and 11, 1957

GALVESTON—Attorney General Will Wilson today filed padlock injunction suits to permanently shut down more than 50 Galveston County gambling joints, bawdy houses, and saloons.

Among the first filed was a suit against the famed Balinese Room and included in the list were more than a dozen other Maceo gambling syndicate establishments on the island and the mainland.

Courthouse workers looked on in amazement as Assistant Attorney General Cecil Rotsch and Jim Simpson, a former FBI agent and Wilson's appointee as special assistant attorney general, carted in a large cardboard box full of petitions in the cases. They were accompanied by a half-dozen state officers.

The cases were filed on the dockets of both District Judges Donald M. Markle and William E. Stone, while a deputy district clerk remarked, "It's a good thing we're getting a third district court soon."

Those places against which the attorney general filed include:

The Balinese Room, Western Room, Moulin Rouge, Mint Club, 419 Club, Playland, Sportsman's Club, Cozy Rooms, Ace Rooms, Esquire Club, Bamboo Club, Pirate Club, Stork Club, Band Box Club, Ciro's, Rainbow Club, Imperial Club, Club Metropole, Omar Khayam, Reno Club, Clock Club, Gulf Towers, Melody Club, Club 88 Keys, Rod & Gun Club, Anchor Club, Idle Hour Club, Tradewinds Club, Jean Davis House, Dickinson

Appendix 183

Social Club, Sylvia D. Lounge, Chili Bowl Bingo Parlor, White House Club, Club C, Beckman's, Ricksha Room, Hurricane Club, Alamo Club, Circle Club, Beach Club, Embassy Club, Palace Club, Streamline Club, Lucky Club, and Acme Rooms.

* * *

Galveston County gamblers, rocked back on their heels and clearly shaken by the surprise power of Attorney General Will Wilson's padlock injunction attack, today were having trouble maintaining their characteristic poker faces.

The gamblers and bawdy house operators are aware that investigators hired by Mr. Wilson and his special assistant, Jim Simpson, have gotten hundreds of pages of evidence on their operations.

They are sweating blood over whether Mr. Wilson intends to be satisfied with civil suits or whether he is heading for a grand jury to get criminal indictments.

* * *

The Maceo Syndicate, it was reported, has cancelled out contracts with headline entertainers who were scheduled to appear at the Balinese Room during the next several months. The place is blacked out, not even serving food, let alone operating gambling.

In the wake of the filing of injunctions against gambling, bawdy house and saloon operations, the Isle seemed to close down another notch Monday night. Some saloons were still open, but gambling and vice operations were at a minimum. Indications were that they will get tighter.

Islanders, particularly those interested in gambling and liquor establishments, were obviously shocked and shaken by Mr. Wilson's crackdown.

Index

(Italic indicates reference to photo)

A
Acree, Deonna, 159-161
Acree, Greg, 159-161
Adelman, Stan, *36*, *49*
Allen, Cary, 59
Allen, Terry, 58
Alvin High School, 145
Alvin Independent School District, 145-148

B
B-26 bomber, 32, 33, 50
Balinese Room, 126, 129, 130, 132, 175, 176, 182
Banister, W. G. "Guy," 86, 87, 92
Barker, Jerry D., 117, 118
Barker, Owen, 117, 118
Barksdale Field, Shreveport, Louisiana, 33, 36, 65
Battle of the Bulge, 50
Beauvais, France, also Beauvais-Tille, 43, 44, 46, 63, 69
Bedichek, Roy, 19, 77
Beeton, Timothy A., 160-161
Bell, Spurgeon, 147
Blythe, California, 29
Bray, Bob, 173
Bristol Hotel, Galveston, 124

Britt, Charles G., 146
Britt, Charles W., 74, 75

C
Campbell, Roy Lee, 29, 30
Carlson, Grace, 91
Cartwright, Herbert, 125, 126
Chicago, Illinois, 84
Citizens Military Training Camp, 3, 25
Clayton, Cy, 17
College of the Mainland, 154-158, 161-163
Communist Party, 85, 87
Convertine, Frank, 62
Cooper, Kathy, 145-148
Cooper, Kathy v. Alvin Independent School District, 145-148
Cooper, Roy, 4, *34*
Copperas Cove Crony, The, 14, 15
Copperas Cove High School, 20
Copperas Cove, Texas, 3
Cordes, Alex Olaf, 67
Coryell County, Texas, 19
Crucifix, Georges, 65

D
Damiani, Jules, Jr., 108
Delorosa, Bennie, 153-154
Dewald, Louis, *34*
Dibrell, Charles G., Sr., 114

186 Flak Bait

Dickinson, Texas, 9, 99
Dobie, J. Frank, 77

E
Eckert, H. K. "Griz," 157-158
Egner, Richard, 150-152
Emmite, Carlo, 164
Escamilla, Manuel, 65-69
Escamilla, Roberto, 68

F
Fargo, North Dakota, 87
Federal Bureau of Investigation, 77, 81-94
First Hutchings Sealy National Bank, 124
Flak Bait, 66, 67
Fort Myers, Florida, 33
Fort Sam Houston, San Antonio, Texas, 73
451st Bomb Squadron, 69
Franklin, John, 113
French Riviera, 60

G
Gallant, Joe, 62
Galveston County Bar Association, 109, 116
Galveston Police Department, 114
Galveston, Texas, 81
gambling, 101, 106, 116, 120-137
Garrison, Homer, 131
Gibson, Hugh, 151
Givens, James D. "Buddy," 121-123, *122*, 136, 173-176
Goldap, William, 76
Goldstein, Ralph, *36, 49*
Gorman, John, x
Green, Bob, 9
Grenock, Scotland, 36
Gunder's Wonders, 66
Gunderson, Herb, 66

H
Hardy, G. P., 146
Harrell, Marvel Simpson, *166*

Henderson, Johnny, 156-158
Hollenbeck, Pat Simpson, *166*
Hollywood Dinner Club, 133
Hoover, J. Edgar, 81, 82, 86, 90, 109
Humble Pipeline Company, Station C, 21

I-J
Ile de France, 36
Jahn, Eddie, 134-136
Johnson, Curtis "Pop," 54-56
Johnson, Marsene, 116
Johnson, Walter, 109

K
Kemah, Texas, 123
Klevenhagen, John, 130
Kugle, Bill, 125, 126, 130

L
Lane, Tom, 124, 125
Le Culot, Belgium, 60
Leavenworth, Simone Simpson, ix, 68, 117, 139, 161, *165*
Lilienstern, Holman, 151-152
Limones, Jesus, 153-154
Longoria, Felix, 42-43

M
MacDill Field, Tampa, Florida, 32
Maceo, Rosario "Rose," 130
Maceo, Salvatore "Sam," 130
Maceo Syndicate, 101, 101, 126, 174
Maersk Container Service Company, 159-161
Markle, Donald, 120, 125, 134, 135, 182
Martin, Rip, 21, 22
Mattax, Tom, *36, 47, 49*
McCann, Everett, 148-150
McNair, Leslie, 58
McSwain, George, 82
McVey, Clyde, 7
Messer, Virginia, x
Metze, Joe, 76
Minneapolis, Minnesota, 86

Index   187

Moody, W. L., 113,114
Moore, Joe, 63, 64
Morgan, Don B., 150

N
National Air and Space Museum, 66, 67
Newcomer, Henry, 46, 55
Nice, France, 60
Nokes, George, 133
Nowell, James, 127
Nye's Annihilators, 38

O
O'Hair, Madalyn Murray, 161-163
Osher Lifelong Learning Institute, ix

P
Palm Springs, California, 29, 30
Palmer, Cecil, 99
Patterson, Albert, 109
Patterson, Dr. Joel, x
Pearl Harbor, Hawaii, 26, 73
Pehr, Bill, 32
Phenix City, Alabama, 108

R
Rain in the Face, 89-91
Reilly, Frank J., 84
Reynold, Joe, 146-148
Roer River, Germany, 59
Rogers, Carol Griffith, *100*
Rosebud Sioux Indian Reservation, South Dakota, 89
Rosson, John, 111, 112
Rotsch, Cecil, 182

S
Salvato, Pete, 164
Samuel, John, 46
Santa Ana, California, 26
Sierpina, Michelle, x
Simler, George, 56
Simpson, Bob G., 2, 3, 4, 25, 28, 72, *138, 166*
Simpson, Connie Griffith, ix, 92-99, *93, 95, 98, 99, 100, 107, 110, 115, 128, 139, 141, 165, 167, 168*
Simpson, Dick, 3, 21, 22, 111, 112, *138, 166*
Simpson, Eva Curtis Green, 4, 9, 12, *138*
Simpson, Gregory Todd, 161, *165*
Simpson, James "Jamie" Griffith, ix, 139, *165*
Simpson, James P., 2, 4, 5, *8*, 14, 27, 34, 36, *41*, 44, *49*, 57, *61*, 72, *83*, 98, 100, 107, 110, 115, 119, 137, *138, 139, 140, 141, 144, 165, 166*
Simpson, Jimmy Alene, 3
Simpson, Joe, 3, *34, 138, 166*
Simpson, Lynn, 3
Simpson, Marvel, 3
Simpson, Scott Wade, 139, *165*
slot machines, 133-134, 175
Smithsonian Institution, 66
Socialist Workers Party, 91
Stallworth, Herbert, 157-158, 161-162
Sterngold, Myron, 40
Stevenson, Adlai, 164
Stone, William E., 120, 182

T
Teague, Paul, 155-158
Texas Centennial of 1936, 16-18
Texas City High School, 150-152
Texas City, Texas, 13
Texas Department of Public Safety, 131
Texas Observer, 172-176
Texas Rangers, 127, 129, 131
322nd Bomb Group, 38
Tyson, Herschel, *36, 49*

U
U. S. Army Air Corps, 22, 25
U. S. Army Corps of Engineers, 134
University Interscholastic League, 19
University of Texas, 20, 68, 105, 117, 163
University of Texas Medical Branch, ix, 108

Utopia, Texas, 21

V-W-Y
Van Flossen, Jennings, *36, 49*
Waco, Texas, 10
Warren, Earl, 146
Weatherly, Tom, 11
Webb, Walter Prescott, 77, 127
Weeks, Chauncey, 58
Wellborn, O. G., 146
Williams, Laurette, 161
Wilson, Attorney General Will, 119, 131, 134, 136, 174, 182
Yaws, Carroll S., 121-123, *122*, 136, 173-176